AMERICAN TANTRUM

THE

DONALD J. TRUMP
PRESIDENTIAL ARCHIVES

AMERICAN TANTRUM

THE

DONALD J. TRUMP
PRESIDENTIAL ARCHIVES

• • •

ANTHONY ATAMANUIK

WITH NEIL CASEY

FOREWORD BY HOWARD FINEMAN

WILLIAM MORROW
An Imprint of HarperCollins*Publishers*

Interior photographs by Deborah Feingold
Map illustration by Dyna Moe

HarperCollins books may be purchased for educational, business, or sales pro-
motional use. For information, please email the Special Markets Department at
SPsales@harpercollins.com.

FIRST EDITION

DESIGNED BY WILLIAM RUOTO

Library of Congress Cataloging-in-Publication Data has been applied for.

ISBN 978-0-06-285188-8

18 19 20 21 22   LSC   10 9 8 7 6 5 4 3 2 1

To my mom, my stepfather, my dad, and my intelligent,
beautiful, and patient wife, Flossie

I alone can fix it.

    —Donald J. Trump

This and no other is the root from
which a tyrant springs; when he
first appears he is a protector.

    —Plato

Contents

Spelunking into the Mind of Trump

by Howard Fineman

The Tang-hued tweet storm that is Donald J. Trump is a fateful challenge to democracy, science, the rule of law and the rational mind. In the struggle to maintain our sanity—and form of government—we need insight into (and comic distance from) our 45th and most infantile, vindictive, insecure, racist, ignorant and hallucinogenic president. Thankfully, for our nation and the world, we have a brilliant improv comic, impressionist, sketch artist, Comedy Central star, and now author to help us understand, survive, and laugh our way through Trump's epic American Tantrum. His name is Anthony Atamanuik and IMHO he is a genius.

Trump is a special test for comedians, including Anthony. Our president is so over the top that no one else's shtick can match him.

He is a mess of contradiction: oafish and yet ominous; openly full of it, yet out to destroy anyone not beholden to him; pathetic, almost pitiable, in proclaiming his insecurities, but furious at those who validate his self-loathing. He is more than vaguely amusing at times, but very rarely in the way he intends. He provokes nervous laughter, ominous laughter. He is the post-post–World War Two–era "strongman" that only America could produce: a pratfall-prone, cartoonish salesman who harbors a goal—sweeping, untrammeled power—that isn't funny.

So we need to laugh, warily. But how? Well, you can play Trump as a cardboard figure with news-of-the-week jokes generated by committee and acted with a few obvious physical gestures. A certain prominent actor does just that, but it is neither very funny nor all that thought-provoking. No, the only way to play Trump is from the inside out; to bravely spelunk into the life and mind of the most powerful infantile narcissist on earth. You have to inhabit him, channel his weaknesses, his desperate desire to be admired, think and react as he does, then take it further over the top than even he would. That's precisely what Atamanuik does so amazingly and amusingly on Comedy Central's *The President Show*, and now in this book, *American Tantrum*, a made-up series of "real life" interviews with and transcripts of The Donald. It could only have been written by someone able to see the world as he sees it and return alive to reveal the dark humor in it.

How does Anthony make what is widely regarded as by far the "best Donald Trump?" One key is improv. He isn't an impersonator, or impressionist. He is an inhabitor—someone who climbs inside a character. That knack, in turn, stems from decades of experience in sketch and improv. Born in Boston to a singer-actor mother and a rock drummer father, Anthony took his childhood living room lounge act to his Cambridge, Massachusetts, prep school. In fifth grade, he told his teacher that he was going to do a skit about the headmaster. The teacher objected. Anthony vowed to do a different skit. Of course, when he got onstage he did the first one. It killed. (He also moved on to another prep school.) At Emerson College in Boston he plunged headlong into improv comedy, continuing to do so in L.A. until he found his true home in New York at one of the country's premier sketch and improv communities, The Upright Citizens Brigade. The UCB's alumni include Amy Poehler, Kate McKinnon, Donald Glover, Aziz Ansari, and Adam Pally. The hit TV show *30 Rock* followed—Anthony was a cast member for nearly seven years.

It also helps that Atamanuik has a feel for politics and for the breadth of the American experience. I know, because we have talked a lot of politics. He knows it cold, and from all sides. In high school, he ran for—and won—the student presidency. As a boy in Boston, he'd hang out in New Hampshire to sample the presidential primary. He befriended Republican Bill Weld in Massachusetts; while working at the legendary John's Pizza restaurant in New York's Greenwich Village, he became friends with New York mayor Rudy Giuliani. After leaving *30 Rock*, Anthony took an odd but useful detour, doing a sketch show called the *B.S. of A*, produced by Glenn Beck's The Blaze website, one of the most popular on the right. "Working on that show was a great lesson in understanding the 'other side,'" he told me, "and understanding the benefit of a healthy tension between right and left in this country."

Of course, Donald Trump isn't into healthy tension. He is into tension, which is enervating for the country and the media, not to mention NATO, but also a source of humor. I first saw Anthony as Trump in—appropriately enough, New Hampshire. It was the 2016 campaign season, on a snowy February night at the Shaskeen pub on Elm Street in Manchester. Trump and Bernie Sanders were on the rise in the state, as it happened, and Anthony and his friend James Adomian had gone on a national road tour with a "debate" between Anthony as Trump and James as Sanders. Real journalists would play "moderator," following a very loose, bare-bones set of topics and intro lines. Wearing deliberately cheap and obvious wigs and makeup, the two would improvise their way through more than an hour of hilarious back-and-forth. The thirty-city tour was a success (I was honored to play moderator once), and the show was recorded live at a theater in Brooklyn. It debuted at number one on iTunes upon its release.

Anthony is now best known for *The President Show,* which launched on Comedy Central in 2017. The idea is pure gold: that the president, fed up with being crushed by the late-night comedy talk shows, hosts his own from the Oval Office, with the ever-pliable Mike Pence, played by Peter Grosz, as his sycophantic announcer and sidekick and Pally as the oleaginous Don Jr. Taped in front of a live audience in Stephen Colbert's old studio, the show is one hysterical bit after another, every one of them full of insight about Trump and the societal wreckage he is causing. But something else struck me in my (wholly superfluous) role as a consultant on the show: the hints of pity, sympathy, and even compassion that Anthony shows for what must be the truly miserable experience of living in the skin of Donald Trump. Much of the country is unhappy, but if it is any solace, so is the president, and there is something ruefully funny about that.

In this new book, Anthony turns his comic imagination—and

by now well-developed sense of how Trump sees himself and the world—to further document his and our predicament. *The President Show* uncannily predicted key moments, including his naïve, supine negotiating moves and ludicrously inflated self-assessments of them; the administration-created immigration mess; and Trump's dismissal of Steve Bannon. Here, the made-up transcripts and interviews are just as funny, and undoubtedly will prove just as prescient. The transcripts include one in which the president demands to be briefed about all of those aliens in Area 51. Bureaucrats on the other end of the phone humor him, assuring him that there is indeed a scary "slimy guy" in the basement. They don't identify him further. I'm guessing his name is Robert Mueller, which would be Anthony Atamanuik's funniest sketch of all.

THE PROJECT

Archivist's Note

Introducing
the Presidential
Pocket Library

Since this is the introduction, I thought I might as well introduce myself. My name is Kelsey Nelson. I am a golf writer (and golf wronger!) turned editor turned columnist. My regular readers can feel free to "play through" this section and get a good table down at the 19th Hole.

I spent fifteen years as an editor at *Golf & Stream* magazine, then ten more as an editor at large (they swear the title has nothing to do with my waistline) writing my monthly column "Mulligan's Wake." My wife, Peg, and I are semi-retired in Florida, where we are members in good standing (and better stumbling) at Mar-a-Lago, the golf club where I first had the pleasure of meeting Donald J. Trump a few years before he became the 45th president of the United States.

To set the scene, it was a beautiful spring Wednesday, about a quarter past happy hour. I was at the edge of the fairway looking for the ball that got away when I heard someone stomping and grunting in the brush. I pushed a branch aside and saw a lumpy man pick up his own ball and toss it back toward the green. That gentleman was none other than Donald J. Trump, owner of the course, celebrity billionaire, and future president of the United States! He tiptoed away before I could introduce myself, but later that night in the dining room I was surprised to feel a hand on my shoulder. I turned around, fully expecting to see an old friend or waiter there to tell me, "You've had enough, Kelsey." But instead there he was again, larger than life: The Donald. This time with a big grin on his face. "Did you see anything today?" I remember him asking. "I don't think so, Mr. Trump. Maybe just the owner of the greatest golf course in the world testing out some new green regulations," I answered with a twinkle in my eye that he promptly returned. And so we became fast friends.

It was a friendship that paid dividends. The Trump Organization started inviting me to cover the openings of their new golf courses for my magazine. Not only did I get to travel all over the world and have first swing (not to mention second and third) at some beautiful virgin links, I also started attending their super luxe VIP charity events (including the one where a guy "won" a hole-in-one contest and went on to greedily sue the Trump Foundation for the money he'd been promised in one of the most unsportsmanlike episodes I've ever encountered; for more details, see my column "Bogey on the Unfairway," September 2012). We lost touch when Mr. Trump started to focus on his political career and his company started focusing on international real estate projects, but when my friend Donald was elected president,

I raised a glass. When he invited me to come to the White House, I nearly dropped one!

It was 8:15 a.m. in Florida a few weeks after the inauguration. My wife, Peg, was sizzling up some turkey bacon while I was reading the newspaper on the NordicTrack. My cell phone buzzed with a call from a blocked number. Fearing yet another telemarketer (see my June 2016 article "PERVERSE Mortgages?") I was going to let it go to voice mail, but something told me to pick up: Peg! (I'm kidding, dear.)

On the other end of the line was the unmistakable New Yawk accent belonging to the 45th president of the United States. He said he had just woken up from a dream that he didn't want to tell me about, but he remembered me and my articles fondly and offered me the position of Presidential Librarian and Archivist on the condition that I could come to Washington, DC immediately and start assembling the documents that would comprise this volume, the first-ever Presidential Pocket Library, which the president insisted we publish before the opening of the Obama Presidential Library in Chicago. Before the bacon was even cold, I had given Peg a kiss and hopped the first flight to our nation's capital where I checked in to a hotel (and made fast friends with the bartenders at the Capital Grille).

The next morning I was asleep in my clothes in my room at the Hilton Garden Inn when my phone rang at nine o'clock on the dot. Expecting to hear the robotic voice of the automatic wake-up call, I gave my best "Frank Nelson" greeting to what turned out to be an unamused man from the Secret Service. He told me that they weren't going to wait for the results of my background check so I could "swing by the White House whenever." As it turns out, the FBI found out that some of the president's best guys had a few lovers' quarrels in their past, so the administration elected to just suspend background checks for everyone. So I devoured some room service eggs, steamed my best polo, and walked H Street to Lafayette Square. There it was, like a postcard brought to life: the White House.

I walked straight up to the gate, where a stray cat was nursing its kittens by the empty security booth. A man with dreadlocks was scaling the fence. He waved to me from the parapet, then dropped to the ground and elbowed the gate open for me before running to the Rose Garden to make the nightly news. I entered gingerly and made my way up the path. Near the West Wing, I took a moment to appreciate the history of the sacred ground on which I was standing (and watch the Secret Service tackle that protester; some of these guys have a future in the NFL!). I heard a creaking sound from behind some bushes and saw a man in a chef's hat light up a cigarette next to an open screen door. I waved hello. "Mind if I come in this way?" I asked. "Sure," he replied with a profanity, "be my guest."

So in I went through the West Wing kitchen, where rows of gourmet chefs were pounding burger patties and sliding racks of them into the freezer. I proceeded to the corridor, which was empty except for a weeping woman in a business skirt, heels clicking down the hallway. I saw another Secret Service agent. I told him I was there to see the president. He shrugged and gestured down the hall. I smelled liquor on his breath, so I made a note to circle back with him later on. As I walked through empty office bullpens, I heard a man screaming at the top of his lungs. A shrill, scratchy gorilla scream from a man who has had practice. I tiptoed to the door and peeked my head through, holding my breath. This was my first glimpse of the Oval Office of the tilted mass of the 45th president of the United States unloading a day's worth of anger on a cowering Steve Bannon, Reince Priebus, and Sean Spicer. As they shuffled out of the room, I stepped in, eager to introduce myself. And the tone changed instantly.

The president sat back in his chair and smiled. "Kelsey," he said. "I heard you said some very nice things about my golf courses." It was like a storm cloud blew out of the room. It felt like it was just the two of us in the whole entire world. I bathed in the warmth and the charisma that I remembered from our previous encounters, now amplified by the trappings of power. Being in a room with Donald Trump is like meeting the uncle you always dreamed of having. We quickly agreed on some ground rules: The archive must be tremendous, I must be the kind of guy he can count on, and don't tell Melania. Tell her what, I don't know. But I agreed to all three.

Now for some full disclosure (don't worry, I'll keep my pants on). I've been called many things in my life, including some choice four-letter words, but nobody has ever said I was a "political" kind of guy. My wife, Peg, is a lifelong Democrat. She volunteered for Mondale when she was twenty-nine (and she's been twenty-nine ever since). I consider myself an Independent, though I usually vote Republican (so I can afford to have a wife!). So if you hadn't guessed already, I did support President Trump in 2016. I was sick of how all the other candidates from both parties had forgotten about people like me: The guys (and gals) who work hard for their families and still think this country is actually pretty great. I don't want to feel bad for having a nice car and a nice house in a nice neighborhood. If having a good life makes me the problem, I'm not sure how eight more years of the Clinton Cabal was going to be the solution.

But let me get off my soapbox here. This book draws from both public and private documents, transcripts of conversations in person and over the phone, interviews, and fun facts which I hope will paint an accurate picture of the unique and historic presidency of Donald J. Trump. Whether you support him or can't stand him, I hope you can put your feet up, crack a cold one, and find something to laugh about (other than my handicap!). After all, in the words of the great Jimmy Buffett, "If we weren't all crazy, we'd just go insane."

CHEERS!

Kelsey Nelson

Interview

_____

The Library

Kelsey Nelson: Mr. President, it's an honor to be here.

President Trump: Look at this guy! Strong guy. Look at you.

K: Thank you, sir. I try to stay healthy.

T: Incredible.

K: So this is our first interview for your presidential library project. I wanted to note a couple of things at the beginning.

T: Very big.

K: Most presidents wait until—

T: You can say it: They die.

K: No, that's not what I was going to say.

T: Yeah, I should call the Secret Service in. You just threatened me.

K: No I didn't, sir.

T: I'm kidding, I'm just kidding. I play, I kid.

K: Most presidents wait until the end of their term as president before they start assembling their presidential library.

T: I think it's an incredible idea to give people a living document. Living document.

K: General Kelly told me that you want to get yours out before Obama's library opens.

T: Unbelievable. This Obama, what right does this guy have to have a library? To open a library, what's it gonna have, Kenyan books? Half Kenyan books? Why does he get to build his library while I'm president? He should have built his library while *he* was president. His time is done. He's putting it in Chicago. And in Chicago there's so much death, so much killing. People can't even go to the play *Chicago*. Because there's so much violence in the balconies. What about the gun deaths there? It's so incredible. People wear their theater blacks to do the show *Chicago*, and then you have theater black on theater black violence, and that's so incredible. Where are you from again?

K: I was born in Cleveland.

T: You want a Coke?

K: No thank you.

T: Look at this. See this button?

K: Yes, I've heard about this, sir. Very charming.

T: You push the button, you get a Diet Coke.

K: Of course. Well there's more to your job than that, I imagine.

T: Yeah, a lot of work. It's a lot of work. Documents, lots of important people to meet, dignitaries, big deals, trade.

K: Yes, sir.

T: Immigration, DACA, healthcare. So many issues. Obama left a mess. A total and complete mess. This place was so disgusting when we got here. There was soot and dust everywhere, and the furniture

was ugly, and let's face it. He killed this country. He ruined this country. I turned the economy around the day I entered office.

K: Yes, sir. Second, most presidential libraries are buildings that they
build. It seems odd to me as a famous builder, someone whose name
is on many buildings—

T: I've built many buildings.

K:—that you would choose to publish your library as a pocket library,
as a book—

T: I can't wait.

K:—not a physical structure.

T: We can't wait. Have you ever heard of a blueprint? You know what
a blueprint is?

K: I do, sir.

T: Blueprint?

K: Yes, sir.

T: A blueprint.

K: Yes, sir.

T: The blueprint is something you do before you make the building.
And that way when you build the building and you lay the foundation, and the contractors start putting the wiring, and all the
important— I know all this stuff, I know all this stuff, because this
is what I do.

K: Yes, sir.

T: I build. You need to make a blueprint. And this book is a beautiful,
beautiful blueprint. One of the most beautiful blueprints. And I can't
wait for a building. As you know, I have totally recused myself from
my businesses. My sons now operate the Trump Organization.

K: Is that exactly true, sir? I mean, you seem to be participating.

T: I recused. I totally recused.

K: Does that have a legal meaning? Because recused is usually in the context of litigation or a trial.

T: I recused. I removed myself. I recused. I recused. That's the right word. Je r'ecuse. What's your outfit?

K: *Golf & Stream* magazine.

T: One of the great magazines, *Golf & Stream*. You keep us away from all the streams, because as we know, you know where all the streams are.

K: Many of them.

T: And we met on the green. The golf green. We became friends the night they cooked the big fish at Mar-a-Lago.

K: That's right.

T: Did you have the fish?

K: No.

T: I'm gonna get somebody to fix that. I'll get someone to fix that. You gotta go down to Mar-a-Lago and get dinner. Have some fun, have some drinks, have a few laughs, you know? Eat the big fish. Go to the Nakatomi Plaza. I'm kidding, I just watched *Die Hard* again last night. These terrorists are terrible people. What they did to the Nakatomi building. Did you get that Coke?

K: Yes.

(A long pause)

K: So, um, I've got a, um—your aides released some documents that I'm going to assemble and edit together into what I hope is a readable, educational, and with some luck, entertaining history of your presidency in progress. And these interviews that we're doing together will be part of that living document.

T: Do you see that bird? Look at that bird out there.

K: That's a big bird.

T: That's a real bird! What is that, a crow?

K: It's a very large crow. Or a raven.

T: That big bird better not come in here.

K: I imagine that's not really possible for the bird, sir.

T: You can never trust the Irish. My father used to tell me that. You got Irish blood, don't ya?

K: Yes.

T: Let me tell you something, never trust the Irish. You people hide under bridges, you people steal babies in the middle of the night.

K: I think that's leprechauns. Or some kind of fairy.

T: That's why we have to build the wall. Tell me about the libraries.

K: Well, have you been to any of them?

T: The libraries?

K: Have you visited Bill Clinton's presidential library in Little Rock?

T: No!

K: Ronald Reagan's in Simi Valley?

T: Yeah, I went in front of it.

K: What about Lyndon Johnson's in Austin?

T: No. Why would I go there?

K: I don't know, sir. Some people go.

T: They shot Kennedy there!

K: In Austin?

T: Yeah!

K: That was Dallas, sir.

T: That was Oswald, I thought.

K: Are you planning, sir, on releasing any more of the Kennedy documents that you've chosen to keep classified?

T: JFK. Blown away. What else do I have to say. Is what Billy Joel said in "We Didn't Start the Fire." And you can go see him for free at Madison Square Garden, you know? He's playing free concerts all the time. So incredible. He's really a great guy. Great piano player. And when I heard those lines—who knows what happened to him? Nobody understands what happened. Nobody knows what happened to Kennedy. And we need to have the truth out. But, at the same time, I have learned from trusted people, very smart people, from very smart people, I mean not as smart as me, but very smart people. I kid, I kid. And they've shown me some documents that I have to redact. We have to redact some of them. Redacting is the act of not bringing in and not showing the document. Named after the winged dinosaur, the Redactatactly. The Rederotactyl. The Redactatacteral. It flew with mighty wings and picked up all the Jurassic animals and dropped them wherever they wanted to go. You ever think about that? A bird with lizard skin? That's crazy! It's like, it's got a big long tongue that can smell, but also fly! Not scarier than a shark. Sharks are the scariest. You ever see a shark?

K: Yes sir.

T: Very frightening.

K: I agree.

T: They got big jaws, and they don't care about what they do. They've been around for like millions of years. Way longer than human beings.

K: That's true, sir.

T: You know, if you ask Mike, he'd say everyone showed up six thousand years ago. The guy's crazy. He believes that there were dinosaurs walking with human beings! Even I know that's not true. Mike's weird. Here's all I'm gonna say: If you have to sit down with Mike, you can have a code word. And if you say it, I'll come in and stop the conversation. Cause that guy's boring. Let me tell ya. But he's got eyes like a shark and he's always moving. Fidgeting. Do you want another Coke?

K: No.

T: Anyway, Kennedy, so there was some information in the documents—we want to release it all, we want the Freedom of Information Act. Fiya-Fiyoah-FOIA. And when we do that, we have an incredible opportunity to make it all available. And some of the things that were redacted were that Jack Ruby had worked for the CIA for two years prior to owning the club. He also had met with Oswald the night before, which put them in the same place, and they knew each other. Another document revealed that George H. W. Bush was stationed in Dallas that day. Some people are saying he was the second gunman, but I'm also hearing he may have been the first. And the reward was the CIA top leadership, after having no documented responsibility at the CIA up until 1976. Oh! And! Then they made him president. Trust me, they would have made him president in 1980. I don't want to get into the Reagan stuff. They made an attempt on him to try to get Bush in office early! Then we would have had the Iran-Iraq war in the mid-80s. Anyway, it's a crazy document, and I wish I could share it. So many incredible things. You married?

K: Yes

T: What's your wife look like?

K: She's a beautiful woman.

T: Sure, sure. I want stats. Blonde? How tall?

K: She's 5 foot 1; she's a brunette.

T: Whoa! Lil spinner.

K: What?

T: Lil spinner.

K: No sir.

T: She spin around like a top?

K: No sir.

T: Pretty hot.

K: Sir, I—

T: I'd like to meet her. Have I met her?

K: I don't think so.

T: I'll meet her. All right, are we done? I like to get my day started by eleven. You can hang around and finish up.

THE DONALD

Archivist's Note

For those of you who haven't been living under a rock for the past thirty years, one of the most intriguing public figures this country has managed to produce is Donald J. Trump, who rose to prominence in the cutthroat world of New York City real estate in the 1980s. Not satisfied with a life surrounded by decadent wealth and beautiful women, he agreed to swap places with me. Oh, was I daydreaming? I mean he decided to enter public service and became president of the United States. But before we learn more about his presidency, I wanted to take this opportunity to learn more about the man behind the man.

For today's interview, the president invited me to join him in the private residence on the second floor of the White House. I held my breath as I walked up the Grand Staircase and into the Center Hall, trying to think of every president since Adams who had retreated here after a long day of tending to the nation's business.

"Kelsey! Kelsey!" came a whisper from the door in the middle of the hallway. "In here!" President Trump was standing on the west side of the Yellow Oval Room near the entrance to the Truman Balcony toeing a chalk line that bisected the room. "You can come across. You can. She doesn't care if I have visitors. People visit. We split the floor. It's a good deal."

He led me through the living room where a half dozen or so copies each of the books the president had co-authored over the years were scattered on the bookshelves. I followed him into the master bedroom where he climbed into his big bed and pulled up the sheets.

EARLY LIFE

Kelsey: So, Mr. President, you're a real New Yorker.

Trump: Through and through.

K: You're the consummate New Yorker. People can't think of New York City without thinking of Donald Trump.

T: They think of New York, they think of Trump.

K: All over the country, when I'd shop at Macy's I'd see your products. Donald Trump mattresses, Donald Trump ties, Donald Trump suits. Everywhere but New York.

T: We're getting there.

K: Well, I want to talk about growing up in the city, sir.

T: I'm so tired!

K: It's two in the afternoon, sir.

T: So tired. When's *Let's Make a Deal* on?

K: I don't know, sir.

T: Okay. I'm gonna find it in the *Guide. The TV Guide*. Remember the

Guide? I loved *The Guide.* They tell me what's on. When I was a kid, I watched some of the best TV. Is that what we're talking about?

K: Well let's start at the beginning. You were born and raised in Queens?

T: I grew up in Queens. I grew up in Jamaica Estates, Queens. Out near Hollis. In Jamaica, Queens.

K: Born in Jamaica, Queens. Very nice. You made it your life's mission to make a splash in New York City real estate.

T: Where is—what—*Family Feud?*! When did they put *Family Feud* on?

K: I think it's on every day, sir.

T: Yeah, but now it's where *Let's Make a Deal* used to be. So now I don't know where *Let's Make a Deal* is.

K: I don't know, sir.

T: Look at this guide. Does it say WGN?

K: Yes, sir.

T: I don't know. I don't watch that *Family Feud.* Steve Harvey . . . good guy, but . . . too much. It's too much. Makes me laugh, I can't think when I'm listening to him. Now here's the thing. I grew up in Queens. I grew up in a very small house—grew up in a very tiny house. My mother and my brother and my sister and my father. My mother! Was a Scottish woman, and she was very tough. They called her the Scottish Angel because of her beautiful flowing red hair. And my dad was even tougher. This was a guy who used to go to work, come home, and he didn't want to be bothered. But what I'll tell you, and this is very true, I'll tell you this only one time, so incredible. I used to go into the neighborhood and play with all the kids. And we had fun, I used to throw rocks at little girls, and wood. We'd play stickball in the ditch. All the New York street games. Grab the Bottlecap. Stink up the Bus Stop. And there was Bucket Ball, you'd put a bucket in the middle of the street and you'd throw a ball in it. And there was Kick the Can, Guess the Asian, Sever the Sissy's Pinky on the Q Train. That's where you'd find the biggest sissy on the train—you can always spot a sissy cause they got a lollipop. Then you'd go up and you'd take some dental floss and just zip! Pull off the pinky. I had a necklace of sissy pinkies when I was a kid. Believe me. I had a very big necklace. But my brother was a real troublemaker. He never wanted to get in line, he was always going for the attention. Always the big guy at school, always the big guy everywhere. And he and Dad used to get in a lot of fights, and my mother would sit in the kitchen going, "Stop it, stop it. Stop it, stop it. Stop it! I'm going crazy, I'm going crazy, I feel myself losing my mind!" And I would hide with my sister, you know my sister's now a great judge. And I would hide with my sister under the bed. My mother and I used to play a fun game called Mommy's Crazy when I would run and hide and my mother would scream, "I'm losing my mind!" and run around the house with a shovel. And then when she got tired and fell asleep, I'd run out of the house. Then I'd go to school and let me tell you, I was not a good kid, I'm not gonna lie. Believe me. I got—they used to call detentions "DTs" for Donald Trump. And I remember my Jewish buddy and I, we used to go up to girls and snap their bra straps. We'd snap their bra straps. And what that does, is they didn't understand I was doing them a favor, because you pull back on their itty-bitty titties, and it makes them stiffer. And that's how I wound up in military school. And I promise you, in the next year of my administration, I will be forming an international community of flat-chested women called the Itty-Bitty Titty Committee. It's a lifelong dream. The Congressional Itty-Bitty Titty Committee will come up with a budget proposal that provides for breast augmentation for all flat-chested women in the United States. Talk to Nunes about it, because I'm not signing any bills. You talk to Nunes about it. Nunes knows everything. Nunes Explains It All!

K: So growing up, did you want to follow your father into business?

T: Well, I mean I followed my father everywhere cause I had to go with him in the car. I kid, I kid. I followed my father into business because my older brother, Fred, he didn't want anything to do with it. He was a fly boy. He'd fly around the world, and he had a bit of a drinking problem. It was very sad, very lonely guy. And every Sunday, they'd have a big fight, my brother Fred and my father. And I was the one who was always there to take care of things. So I'd bring my daddy lunch at work and I'd go with my father, and I remember one of my earliest—this is so incredible—one of my earliest experiences—and family's so important—that's why I work with my sons, that's why I work with my daughter—and I don't work with all of them, but the ones that are important. And I went with my daddy to Ocean Parkway and we had to throw people out. And listen, it was a lot of blacks. It was a lot of blacks. It was a lot of Latinos. And these people, living in squalor! Just living in total squalor. So disgusting. I felt bad for these guys! I felt for these people. But they had to go. And my father was trying to change the community. And this is why I said, what have you got to lose, because I saw how bad it was for the blacks, firsthand. And that was before the Warriors took over the subway system!

K: Your father encouraged you.

T: He encouraged. He encouraged. Daddy said, "You know what, you're the best. You're the most tremendous, you could do so much more than me. Move into Manhattan, take it over." "Dad, I'm so weak, Dad, no!" He said, "I can't do it, son. I can't go to Manhattan." I said, "Daddy, no!" And his body disappeared. And now he just sits with me, and he says, "You can do it, Donald. Lose yourself, Donald. Grab that woman, Donald. Build the building." So that's why in the late 1970s, I started investing in properties around Manhattan and built the Trump name into the empire it is today. And just like the rebels, we're now the empire. 588–2300 empire! And all our carpets are Empire carpets. And if you go to the very top of Trump Tower, you'll see that there is a giant dome. And it's designed so beautifully by this incredible guy who designed a perfect dome that reflects sound. And I built that in honor of my mother. And my mother can go up there any time she wants any time, day or night, and she can scream to her heart's content, and it will echo throughout the city. And all through time! And hopefully, someone, like Jesus or someone, will hear her time screams and come to the future and save us from ISIS. My mother was a screamer. She was known for it. For her ninetieth birthday, we had a map commissioned of all her favorite places to go and scream. She loved to scream. Take a look! They still use it as a place mat in some diners out there in Queens.

TUBE TIME: SHOWS I LOVED GROWING UP

Below is a reconstruction of a *TV Guide* showing a typical night of television President Trump watched as a child. Unbelievably, many

records from that early era of television have been lost since there was no economical way to record broadcasts before the invention of videotape. So we depend on the sharp memories of amateur TV historians like the president, and can only wonder what other great programs that we have absolutely no record of might have been forgotten and forever lost.

HOW DOLL DO THIS? (7 P.M.)

In every episode the ventriloquist was surprised by his little wooden man's tricks, but he was never pleased. No matter what new skills he learned, the little wooden man could never make the big man in the gray hat proud of him. He'd dance and sing and bring friends around, but at the end of the day he'd end up back in his box, his oak eyes cracking with the effort of trying to push out a tear. Sad!

DYKE VAN DICK (7:30 P.M.)

One of the greats.

THE UNDERWATER PRIEST (8 P.M.)

This guy could swim underwater and no one knew he could, but he was a priest and he solved mysteries.

NOZO THE UNCLE (8:30 P.M.)

This was a show where everyone's favorite funny uncle would come from the city and transform into a playful clown whenever the boy's parents were downstairs.

MY TWO SONS I HATE (9 P.M.)

This was the story of a suburban dad smoking his pipe on the porch watching his two sons have a fistfight over a lie he'd told them.

HELP, MY HUSBAND IS A WARLOCK! (9:30 P.M.)

A woman marries a man who turns out to be the kind of magician who bought his tricks from the devil. And she never gets help. No one ever helps her.

HERPE THE CAR WITH VENEREAL DISEASE (10 P.M.)

It was a car that was all white and once in awhile these awful sores would open up on it. And that was the show!

THE MOTHER'S BROTHERS (10:30 P.M.)

This was ahead of its time by about twenty years. It was a variety show. One of a kind. The two brothers hosted it. And they sent their mother to die in Vietnam and they couldn't forgive themselves. So they hosted a show where they used skits and music to hold each other responsible for their mother's death.

THE EVENING NEWS WITH BRONSON CASH (11 P.M.)

Bronson would smoke two packs of cigarettes every night over the course of a broadcast until you could barely see his suit. We watched every night during the McCarthy hearings as his ashtray piled up, a mountain of wet tobacco casting a shadow on his desk. Until his last broadcast, when Bronson stood up, poured kerosene on all those old cigarettes, and, with words that will echo through history, lit himself on fire, shrieking, "How's this for decency?" as the whole studio burned down. The statue of Prometheus at the Rockefeller Center Ice Rink marks the spot where they found his head.

THE TONIGHT NEWS WITH GUS VAN HARVEY (12 A.M.)

This news man was the most famous Quaker since the Oatmeal Pig. Gus always told the truth, and "he didn't care who was listening," which was the slogan of his program in the '50s, Woody Allen's "Radio Days." Gus was America's conscience during the Korean War and a gentleman of the old school: He'd threaten his wife on the air, signing off with a warning that he was coming home in a mood, so she'd better watch her step. I learned a lot from him.

THE LATE LATE NEWS WITH SPIT BRUNCKLE (1 A.M.)

A real muckraker! Spit and his crew weren't afraid to get their nose in the sawdust, digging up stories about everyone from tavern boys and oyster girls to grimy beat cops and women of a certain age. I remember Spit's gin-soaked southern drawl calling for a nuclear first strike against every country he could pronounce.

A LEADER
COMES OF AGE

NEW YORK MILITARY SCHOOL JOURNALS

Homesickness

SEPTEMBER 4, 1959

It was a long ride up here. I'm already missing my old shithole in
Queens. It was a typical day when I finally left; Dad was screaming
and choking Fred while Mommy was crying in the kitchen. It was
hard to leave, but I had to. I gave my brother a sucker punch goodbye
and was out the door! Boy, I'm sure gonna miss my family. I have a
sister too.

School Spirit

SEPTEMBER 14, 1961

People always compare our school to West Point, but does West
Point have an apple orchard AND a pumpkin patch? NO! Last week
I took a wagon ride out to a cornfield and saw a scarecrow ghost! Then

I found a corn maze. I made it to the middle in record time. So easy, just walk through the corn walls to the center! Following a maze path is for losers. That's how General Cornwall Jackson got his name, he walked right through that corn wall and killed all the Indians while yelling "surprise!!!" Shove it up your ass, West Point!

Leadership

OCTOBER 13, 1961

I was put in charge of my first unit today! I've discovered that if I claim absolute authority but delegate all responsibility, I can spend the day watching TV and people will be too scared to ask what I'm doing. I built a hammock by tying my bunkmates' clothes together. It's incredible! I just lie there and watch *Calvin and the Colonel.*

OCTOBER 10, 1962

I did it! I've been promoted from the commander of A Company to an even more powerful post sitting at a desk. Everyone says that I did such a great job commanding these easily bullied freshmen that I'll never be put in charge of anyone again!

Role Models

MAY 5, 1963

I've been reading a lot about Howard Hughes. I really admire his tremendous business mind and obsessive attention to detail: from keeping jars of piss to worrying about nuclear fallout polluting his bones, this guy's cracked the code! As the recent recipient of the New York Military Academy's highest honor, The Neatness and Order Medal, I might even be able to teach him a thing or two! I don't know if my military school experience is preparing me for combat, but I am learning how to keep a clean room with tight bedsheets which qualifies me to work at any Westin in the world.

Brothers-in-arms

SEPTEMBER 20, 1962

I made so many friends when I arrived: Bucky and Spuds and Brooklyn. But one of the great tragedies of my time at the Academy was losing my friend Roger. He caught me getting sweet with myself using a picture of his girlfriend. I'll never forget the look in his eyes, and his last words: "Jesus, Trump, what are you doing?" And like the old saying goes, "Young cadets don't die, they just back away slowly out of the room and ask for a transfer."

The Drill Instructor

APRIL 12, 1962

That drill instructor is a real meanie. So I got a job at the mess hall and I'm slowly poisoning him.

DECEMBER 8, 1962

The drill instructor finally died! Unbelievable!

Becoming a Man

JANUARY 21, 1963

I finally did it! All my towels and sheets are folded perfectly. I'm finally a soldier.

Letters from Home

MARCH 4, 1963

I got a letter from Dad today. He told me the Androgottis down the street are dumping their garbage out on the sidewalk. Why won't any of his soft, fat-fingered sons do something about it? The neighborhood's changing. Love you, Pop.

The Kennedy Assassination

NOVEMBER 22, 1963

Kennedy was shot today. Not surprised, he had a very big head. Easy target. They say this Poindexter, Oswald, shot him. I'm not buying it.

Vietnam

APRIL 9, 1964

Apparently Vietnam isn't just a luxury vacation destination, it's also a slowly developing colonial conflict. My feet hurt.

Graduation

MAY 15, 1964

Graduation day! I got a note from Dad: One day without a failure doesn't make you not a failure. More of that understated German wit. I love you, Daddy!

Archivist's Note

An Evening with General Mattis

One Tuesday night in autumn after the president had screamed his face red at two cabinet members (who resigned, leaked, and were then forgotten) General Kelly pursed his lips and clicked his castanets, thereby directing everyone present to make their exits, and quickly!

After the rush I found myself in an unfamiliar corridor, hastily sorting my notes and dreaming of the Caesar wrap whose crunch was waiting for me back at the Garden Inn, when I heard the jagged hoot of men's laughter echo off the marble. Following the sound, I peeked my head through an open door into a fire-lit lounge where General Mattis sat sipping brandy with some off-duty Marine Security Guards. "Where were you in Vietnam?" he barked when he saw me, showing his teeth. "M-M-Masters in English," I stammered. "Graduate school? Deferment!" The men all laughed. As my face turned red, I darted my eyes toward the waning fire and the painting of the

Kalmar Nyckel sailing above the hearth. But Mattis gestured for me to join them yet, offering me a glass of the sweet stuff.

"Some of the most terrifying stories I know from that godforsaken jungle are from men who never went," he whispered. Each of us leaned in about a foot and a half and inhaled sharply. "Perhaps the one I remember best was told to me by the president himself. I'll tell it to you now as I heard it from him. But drink up, boys, for these words are keen to stay with you for life."

He leaned back and held up his hand, speaking the president's words while moving his fingers like a puppet's mouth until we all got the picture and he stopped.

APOCALYPSE OW: DONALD TRUMP'S PIED-NAM

Fifth Avenue seemed to be going on forever. The cab was moving slowly. The traffic was backed up from a parade for the Mets that was going on downtown. I was so hot. The sticky slime that was forming under my belly paunch was starting to have a scent of its own. And I'll take it. I'll take that smell over the rotten garbage streets of New York City in the '60s. There's a creep that happens in your mind. A slow bleed with visions of torture, foot pain like you've never experienced, permeating your body. I wasn't going to tell them. I wanted to fight. I wasn't gonna be the messenger. No, no. That wasn't my job. I was a soldier. And my feet were the infantry. I couldn't tell them cause I couldn't tell myself.

Aaaah! The spur! The spur burned! As the cabbie slowed to

a halt at the traffic light I took off my shoe and looked at the pulsing lump. Removing the shoe was difficult. It was squeezed over my foot, which had expanded in the heat. Round and hard, the throb, the throb. The ache, the sharp pain of the spur. I don't want anyone to find out about you, spur. Get back in the sock! But you can see it, pressing out, almost as if it had eyes, and it was staring back at you. "You'll never fight, Donald. You'll never fight anything but me."

Suddenly the cabbie spoke up. "Say, blood, you goin' all the way downtown, jive-ass turkey?"

I said, "Yeah, so cool, man. I thought I already told you where I was going when I got in the cab, my brother."

"Yeah, well, there's a lot of traffic, blood. You wanna hit up on the down low?"

"What?"

"You wanna go through Times Square?"

"Sure."

"Get nasty?"

"Yeah, I'll get nasty." Now we were deep in the heart of it. Look at the filth. Was this what our boys were dying for over there? The signs were hanging, looming over the square, the shadows reaching long. Who knew what was down those street paths, guys leaving porn shops with their dicks still out, little pricks lighting up the streets like fireflies. The hookers with their big hair smoking cigarettes, looking at the man in the suit in the cab. They were looking at me, they were seeing inside me lust, a lust and a passion, but it wasn't for them. It was for service.

My spurs were working against me. They were my own Viet

Cong, right in my feet. Lying in wait at night, stinging me with pain. I thought about chopping them off. Then I could get a nickname like "Stubbs" in the military. But they wouldn't take me without feet. I knew I had to go.

The cab jumped the curb and slammed right into the front of the recruiting office in the middle of Times Square. A fire hydrant opened and shot a fountain of water in the air. Clean, cleansing water, water that flowed over me like I was a stone, water that made me white and clean, water that covered the cab and flowed wherever it could go, water that went into the military training center, water that interrupted the cabbie's cries of "Oh dayummmm, oh dayummm!"

I heard the mocking laughter of my spurs. "Water won't stop us." The spurs whistled. They whistled a little tune that I came to know as the spurrfolk had since the age before:

In the valley of the arch
In the wrinkled sands
Grows a li'l lump
That has no hands!

Onward! A determined march
skin nor bone could not deter
It raises up a ruddy bump
Hi ho we greet the little bone spur!

It toils away singing a little tune.
"Bumpy, lumpy, humpy Glur!

"Turdy, lurdy gurdy Whir!

"I am you and you are me.

"My voice is yours and now

  "You're free!

"Moany, groany boney Spur!

"Hiddly Diddly Pap."

The little lump finished its tune and danced all the way back to White Plains, where it lived in a little Spur Hole. Time stretches and snaps in this place. I had no way of knowing how long I'd been talking to the recruiter.

He leaned forward and asked, "What was that song?"

"I didn't sing it."

"Yes you did."

"No, my bone spurs sang it! Are you ready to see my secret? Can you hear my secret? Can I trust you? Are you an assassin?"

"No, I'm an army recruiter."

"My bone spurs are singing. They don't want me to join. They say that war is just another of man's futile efforts to control nature. That ultimately we're just simple animals: Monkeys, tigers, giraffes, preying on one another. Sharp-eyed apes and dull wall-eyed sharks. All of them chasing each other, in an endless cycle of destruction and rebirth. I'm not going to Vietnam, because my daddy says I don't have to."

"What's that?"

"I'm not going to Vietnam, because my daddy says I don't have to. Those were the bone spurs speaking; they're Daddy!"

I felt the bone spurs move all the way up into my throat. And they started talking for me! "I'll ruin you. I'll destroy you. I'll kill your whole family. You know who my dad is? My dad is Fred Trump and I'll ruin you! I got tons of money, you stupid simpleton! You're nothing but a meat sack that's ready to get peppered with bullets and we all know it, you're a human flesh shield!"

Then he signed my form, and I said, "Thank you!" And it was straight to Rockefeller Center to the Rainbow Room, where suddenly my bone spurs felt perfectly fine, so I had a wonderful night out with a beautiful woman named Shelley Duvall.

Finished with the story, Mattis stood up. "Okay, everybody. See you tomorrow."

ALUMNI CORRESPONDENCE

December 7, 2011

Dear Mr. Trump:

Thank you for your recent donation of the multiple copies of your book *Think Big and Kick Ass in Business and in Life* to the New York Military Academy. While we are happy to include works from our alumni in our campus library, we will be unable to accommodate your request of a receipt indicating the value of your gift of a "new curriculum" being worth $12 million. We trust you will be satisfied with the enclosed receipt valuing the book at its cover price of $29.95.

Sincerely,

Col. Bart Karels (Ret.)
Dean of Alumni
New York Military Academy

August 12, 2016

Dear Mr. Trump:

We are writing in response to your most recent letter to remind you that we, in fact, never feature alumni on the cover of our monthly newsletter intended for the young men enrolled in our school. A brief, informal consultation with our board of directors affirms that our organization would have minimal interest in starting a new publication for the purpose of promoting our alumni, their business interests or entertainment ventures. Also, despite your kind offer to rename our "bullshit buildings," we are content to have our campus facilities continue to bear the names of the great tacticians of history: Washington, Patton, Napoleon, etc.. It would be inappropriate and confusing to have our cafeteria named after "Don Jr.," for example. People wouldn't know who we were talking about. Also, apropos of nothing, a man has been calling from pay phones in New York City making similar suggestions for our newsletter and building names, and we wish he would stop.

Sincerely,

Col. Bart Karels (Ret.)
Dean of Alumni
New York Military Academy

January 8, 2017

Dear President Trump:

We are pleased to send you the limited-edition first issue of New York Military Academy's alumni magazine, *Alumnarama!"* which it is our great privilege to inform you features none other than you, Donald J. Trump, the 45th president of the United States, as our first cover story. Our board, by unanimous vote in a formal meeting, has made your most recent suggested changes to the names of our buildings and to our curriculum and sends their warm congratulations. We hope you enjoy the publication and will consider visiting us soon!

Sincerely,

Col. Bart Karels (U.S. Army, Ret.)
Dean of Alumni
Eric & Don Jr. Tough Guys Good Boys Academy

THE VIEW FROM
THE TOP

Trump: You want anything? You want little hot dogs?

Kelsey: Sure.

T: It's little hot dog day!

K: You just have these in a drawer?

T: Yeah. They put a fresh bag of hot dogs in here every day, warmed in a plastic bag.

K: Oh, like a steam bag and they dump it in here?

T: Yeah, and then I use a little toothpick and I pull them out. I love that water. They say hot dog water's good for your health!

K: Yes sir. Well, sir, I have to tell you I'm having a great time sorting through some of your documents here and we found a little trunk full of newspaper clippings about you from the '80s.

T: The 1980s.

K: You know, you were in the *New York Post* more than any other person back then.

T: That's right.

K: And it seemed like you were having a heck of a time.

T: Those are great days, lots of fun. We had great time. We had a great time in the 1980s. Ronald Reagan and the DeLorean where he took a bullet and the *luftballons* and all the other fun things that happened.

K: We found a lot of pictures of you with some beautiful women out at clubs and enjoying the night life.

T: The Night Life. I'd go to Studio 54 and I'd hang out with all the hot celebrities. And see all the great people, and I'd rub up against them. And it was a wild time. A lot of wacky people. But the truth was, I was a builder. I meet a lot of people today, and I go, "I think I gave a hot one to your mommy." And they look at me and they say, "You probably did." And they all love that. Did you see the pictures of me on the bed?

K: Yes sir, I did.

T: I did a lot of those poses. I always loved being sideways on a bed. Laying there with my robe loose. I think it's a beautiful portrait of me at my most relaxed. I don't get time to relax, especially in the 1980s, there was no time to relax. Because I was building an empire.

K: Yes sir.

T: My father could never accomplish what I accomplished—

K: You brought the family business into Manhattan, sir, and you really made a splash.

T: We were a huge splash. Everywhere. All the buildings, all the women. And you see me with all the beautiful women. Suzanne Pleshette. Judith Light. So incredible. All the great women. Margot Kidder. The original Lois Lane. I remember visiting the set of *Superman II* and we had a wonderful time. Chris Reeves, great guy. Big horse guy, and of course the horses undid him in the end. And I warned him, I knew it was gonna happen. I said, "You're riding loose, you're riding fast, Chris!" But he wouldn't listen to me. And I said that to him in 1982! Where do you ride horses anywhere in New York? Except in Central Park. But that's in a carriage. The bridal path. Jackie O. And of course the ghost that rode that horse during Kennedy's funeral. The same ghost that rode the horse in Lincoln's funeral! And not a lot of people know that. It was the same ghost.

K: You know, you bought the Plaza and then you sold it at a loss during this time. Wasn't the Plaza meant to be the crown jewel of your empire?

T: As you know, the Plaza was an incredible purchase. But the thing was that Leona—I mean, that woman—she was a tough lady. And I'd mix it up with the best. You know, a woman like Leona Helmsley, usually you'd see her and go, "Whoa, boy. Whoa! There's a witch! Hold still and grab a garlic." But with Leona, she filled up a room. And she had a powerful way of negotiating and doing business. So you could never underestimate Leona. I purchased it at too high a price point, and unfortunately we had a lot of problems with the plumbing and the electric in the building.

And at the time, let's face it, Central Park was someplace you didn't want to be. You had the Central Park Five roving the park murdering and raping anyone they could find. And it was only when I took a full-page ad out that they stopped. I did the same thing for Son of Sam in the 1970s. And if the paper had listened to me and put the ad out, that dog would have stopped telling him to kill. And it would have said

"Love!" instead. It wasn't the dog's fault. And so we settled in, I put my offices in the Plaza because of course Trump Tower's being built at the time and speaking of time, from my office I would always hear this clock, ticking, ticking, saying, "Tick—tock-tick-tock-tick-tock" and I'd say, "What the hell is that?" and my staff would say, "What?" and I would say, "Is there a clock in here? Where's the clock?" and then I'd hear it singing, "Welcome to our world tick tock welcome to our tick tock welcome to our world of toys tick tock tick tock." And I'd say, "I'm losing my mind!" But after a few weeks I found out it was just the old FAO Schwarz clock across the street, which is gone now, because kids stopped playing with toys and Schwarz couldn't keep up with the iPad or the Nintendo—or us.

K: So you went from a small-time real estate developer to building an empire. This is when you wrote your first book, *The Art of the Deal*.

T: *The Art of the Deal*. One of the great books. I loved it so much. When I read it finally, I said, "I can't believe I wrote this!" And it was true. I wrote *The Art of the Deal* because I wanted everyone to know the secrets, because I have nothing to hide. And here's the thing: I was giving it away for free! I'm giving it away for free. I mean, you had to pay for the book, of course, right? You gotta pay for the book. But once you get the book, it's all in there! It's totally free. And all that information, anybody could do it! I gave everybody a blueprint on how to buy massively depressed real estate in Manhattan. And there was a lot of it. I used to teach a class at the Learning Annex! I would go there and I'd say, "Welcome back! Your dreams were your ticket out," and the studio audience would clap and I'd say, "Okay, Sweathogs! It's time for you to learn about how the real estate is done." And because of that I got on TV. And the truth is, there was a lot of great

television: *Diff'rent Strokes, Facts of Life, Mama's Family.* So many
great shows. *Kids Are People Too, People Are Talking.* All the great ones.
Donahue, and I mean I never missed a *Donahue.* Donahue had me on
two or three times a week. I was one of the great guests. I like to say
to Phil, "Your hair was black when you started, and gray by the time
I was done with you." Because I stressed the guy out. I used to show
up a lot and boy—his wife Marlo Thomas—what a beauty. She was a
real hippie but she was a real beauty. And of course, Danny Thomas's
daughter. And that's almost like doing Danny Thomas! Which would
be a dream. He was a great talent. Finally I told Donahue, "I gotta
walk it back. Because I'm on too much, and what's gonna happen
when they rely on seeing me. It's your show, Phil." And that was it.
And then it was off to *Oprah*!

K: You started getting a lot of press.

T: Yes, but you couldn't because in the early '80s they had the rotary
phones. But by the late 1980s, of course, they had the push-button
phone. I remember a day when you called the operator up and you
said, "What are you wearing? What's going on, honey?" And all
the operators were beautiful, of course because you were imagining
them because you were just hearing the voice. So you'd imagine who
they were, and you'd have a good time. When you were lonely, you
wouldn't even need to go down to Forty-Second Street or hide in the
dressing room at the Bamberger's. You'd call the operator, and you'd
keep her on long enough, and then you'd get your little bust. And then
you'd go, "Connect me to somebody! Cause I'm very lonely!" I used to
spend hours talking to the operator. She was my best friend. And then
I learned there was more than one!

K: Speaking of Forty-Second Street, you know, a lot changed in New

York—

T: *(singing)* Forty-Second Street!

K: A lot changed in New York in the '90s.

T: Forty-Second Street used to be a place for bums and whores and people who dealt drugs. But Rudy cleaned it all up. But let's face it, you had a lot of ghetto kids stealing hubcaps, you had a lot of heroin addicts, you had a lot of jerk places. I went into a movie theater once to go see an incredible *Ben Hur* screening. I love *Ben Hur.* But I fell asleep, and when I woke up, there were two guys doing it on the screen. Potholes. Squeegee guys. You could do whatever you want to a squeegee guy. I mean, those guys aren't even citizens. They're animals. So sometimes they'd squeegee, and I'd go, "You want a ride in the limo?" And we'd have fun. And I'm just doing to the immigrants what Rudy did to the squeegee guys. You say, "Get out of here!" And where are they, where are they now? Nobody knows. They're squeegeeing somewhere, probably in Syria, or in Afghanistan. There's plenty of places to squeegee. We don't need to do it in New York. The Statue of Liberty was something I tried to buy, but then they told me I couldn't! What an incredible penthouse apartment in her head. You have this beautiful apartment in the top of her head—it's already a totally hollow place, build it out like a building!

K: Why did you focus so much on New Jersey and Florida during this time?

T: I knew that New Jersey and Florida were cheaper places to build, one. So incredible. Two, in New Jersey, let's just face it, you had the guys, the connected guys, very easy to get building permits. And I wanted to expand because I felt more at home. I did a lot of business in Atlantic City with those guys. Because in A.C. you bet big, you cash out, you go home, or you go bankrupt and then go home. Either way somebody foots the bill, you end up at home and it feels like home because it is.

Now, Florida, I'll never forget it. I flew down to Florida, I was driving around, the driver was in the front seat, and we're driving past all the big properties in Palm Beach, all of them. And they're so incredible. And the guy says, "Mr. Trump," you know, cause they all talk to me, and I talk to them, he goes, "Mr. Trump." And I say, "Call me Donald," and he says, "No, I know that's a trick." And I say, "It's not a trick!" He says, "Mr. Trump," I go, "Swear to god, call me Donald." And he goes, "Okay, I'll call you Donald." And I go, "You're tricked. Call me Mr. Trump." Then he says to me, "What places ya looking at?" I said I wanted something big. I wanted to buy a bunch of condos and string them together but I couldn't find a property that could do that. And then he mentioned Mar-a-Lago. Said it was a sprawling place. And I go, "I gotta see it." I went to see it and I fell in love. I knew this was a place where I could put too much furniture, tapestries on all the walls, and weird oil paintings of myself in every room. And I did.

Mar-a-Lago is my first love. It's a woman in every way. She's wet and salty. She's by the sea. Warm interiors that keep you comfortable. A place that feeds you and keeps you comfortable at night. And fun to say. Mar-a-Lago. Mar-a-Lago. None of my wives quite had it right. That perfect combination of vowel and L. And she'll live on forever. And apparently it means something in another language. It means "Don't take my house!" in Indian. By the late '80s, neon was all the rage. People were starting to wear bright colors. Electric colors! Shoulder pads. People were rollerblading instead of roller skating.

And then the wall came down and it was the saddest day of my life. There's nothing more sad than when a wall goes down, and ever since then I've wanted another wall to go up. And that's why I wanted to try to buy the Berlin Wall and put it on the southern border of the United States. And who knows—and we'll see what happens in November of 2020 when I take pieces of the Berlin Wall and pieces of the World Trade Center and turn them into the wall that will end this country. At last, the end. Have you ever been in love?

K: Yes, of course. I'm married.

T: I've loved. Loved and lost. Loved and found. I got around. I had a little bit of fun. I had a little bit of fun. Hold on, I wanted to get this going. Hold on.

K: You're making a call?

T: No, just turning the ringer off. On? Off. Go ahead, ask me, ask me about the women.

K: Well, it sounds like you were a real playboy back then.

T: Is your wife around? Is your wife here?

K: No she's not, sir.

T: You wanna go to DC Tits? You been to DC Tits?

K: DC Tits, sir?

T: Yeah, it's a topless club.

K: No sir.

T: In a black neighborhood.

K: I'm all right, sir. I'd really like to get through the book today.

T: Wanna hop on a plane and go to Colorado Cummies?

K: What's that?

T: That's a club out in Denver.

K: Oh. No sir, I'd really prefer not to.

T: Really, I could get some girls out there.

K: I'd like to stick to the task at hand, sir.

T: You want some girls? Come on.

K: No sir.

T: You'd do it.

K: No sir.

T: You'd do it.

K: No sir. Maybe another time.

T: Hear that, honey? Hear that, baby? Hello?

Peg Nelson: Yeah, it sounded like he said "another time maybe," in a polite way.

T: Your husband's cheating on you! Why don't you fuck me then, huh? He's cheating on you, do me!

PN: I don't think he is, Mr. President.

T: I'll give you $200,000 at the end of it and treat you like a whore.

PN: No sir, that's really not what I'm about.

T: Really? You sure?

PN: Yes.

T: Your voice doesn't sound like that. Your voice sounds like you're all about it.

K: Sir, I think we should end this here.

T: You're married to this guy, right? He drinks, you know. I don't drink. I have fun but I don't drink.

PN: Honey?

T: I'm joking, I'm joking, we're having fun.

K: You can go, Peg.

PN: I'm going to hang up.

T: No, you hang up first!

PN: I will.

T: No, you!

PN: I am.

T: You first!

K: She hung up, sir.

T: I have a new crush!

CALL: JOHN BARRON AND PAGE SIX (10/5/1991)

Trump: Hello? Hello? John Barron here. Is this Page Six?

Page Six: Yes it is.

T: It's John Barron.

P: Hello, Donald.

T: Excuse me? Hello, what?

P: Oh. Hello. Mr. Trump.

T: What?

P: Hello, Mr. Trump.

T: He's not here.

P: *(sighing)* Okay.

T: You wanna talk to Donald Trump?

P: If he's available.

T: I'll see if he's available but first I want to tell you something that's so incredible, I mean this is really incredible. I don't know if you've seen the stories or you report on the stories, or you've seen anything about this, uh, Donald Trump, great man, one of the great men, great guy, great builder in New York City, very valuable, lots of money, lots of prestige—

P: I know who you are.

T: So incredible—

P: I know who you are.

T: John Barron, that's who I am.

P: I've talked to you and your boss a number of times.

T: Don—he's one of the best bosses. Great guy. Incredible holdings. He has some great holdings. And a little birdie told me—a little birdie whispered in my ear—and that's hard, because when a birdie whispers in your ear, they're pecking in it. You have to hold very still and let him whisper because his beak will pierce your eardrum. If you twitch, he'll fly away and you'll never know the secret. Are you listening?

P: I'm listening.

T: Be very still. Donald Trump is going to dinner with none other than *Kate & Allie*'s Susan Saint James tonight!

P: Okay, thank you.

T: Susan Saint James, incredibly beautiful woman—

P: I know who she is.

T: *Kate & Allie*, one of the hit shows on television.

P: Where are you dining tonight?

T: *Kate & Allie*, a sitcom about two women, single women, trying to make it in their lives and they're so strong.

P: I know the show.

T: Strong women. And they've got the other one from *SNL*. Who's the other one. Jane Curtin. She's funny. But let's face it, she's gotta be funny. Let's face it. Trump gets the best one. Susan Saint James. He went to a taping—he went to a taping, and I'm just gonna tell you what happened. Donald Trump went to a taping, flew out to Los Angeles and went to a taping of *Kate & Allie*, and after the taping, he charged down the steps, and people are saying, "What's this guy doing? Where's this guy going?" Jumped over the railing, ran onto the studio stage, screaming, "Susan! Susan! Susan! Susan! Susan!" And everyone realized, "This is Donald Trump." And I was there, I was John Barron and I had the same suit and glasses and it's true. It turns out they weren't done shooting. And Trump had ruined the main scene that they had tried to shoot fifteen times! So Donald said, "You gotta go to dinner with me. You gotta go to dinner with me. You gotta go to dinner with me." And eventually Susan Saint James started to cry and shake and said, "Fine, I will." And we never did, but we would have had an incredible meal.

P: Mr. Trump?

T: Hello? Oh—

P: Thank you for the call.

CALL: JOHN BARRON AND *FORTUNE* MAGAZINE (6/7/1996)

Trump: Hello, this is John Barron.

***Fortune* magazine:** Yes, I had several messages from this number?

T: Yeah, uh, you wanted to reach my client—as you know, I'm Donald Trump's publicist.

F: Oh, you represent Mr. Trump?

T: I represent Mr. Trump. An incredible guy, incredible businessman, as you know, he's a great guy and, uh, of course you know there've been a lot of rumors lately, a lot of rumors, about his worth, his financials.

F: I haven't heard anything.

T: Well, apparently there have been a lot of rumors about his worth.

F: I haven't heard anything.

T: You know, what assets are liquid—

F: I haven't heard people talk about this at all.

T: Yeah, well, uh, I'm here to call and tell you that people are talking about it.

F: I haven't heard.

T: Well, you're hearing it now!

F: Well, it sounds like bad news anyway. You're telling me you represent Mr. Trump and he doesn't have a lot of liquidity?

T: No, I have incredible liquidity—I mean, he has incredible liquidity.

F: The fact that you're bringing it up raises questions about it for me.

T: No, excuse me. Excuse me. He has incredible liquidity. He's liquid all over the place. He makes liquid, he's got liquid. He's got a lot of jars. He's liquid all over the place. He's liquid everywhere.

F: All right, well, good to know.

T: And—excuse me—

F: I'm just not sure what this call is in response to. You left me several messages.

T: Mr. Trump wants to be included on the Fortune 500 list and he's been overlooked because—you know he stands to make a serious amount of money, an incredible amount of money. A lot of money, more money than you could imagine.

F: Well, we could get him on the list next year.

T: No, this year. This year he made it.

F: You said he "stands to make it."

T: No, he's making it now. He's making it right now!

F: Look, I mean, these lists are for fun, you know?

T: No!

F: It's good publicity, I understand your position—

T: Excuse me! No! My position—it's not my position, it's Donald Trump's position.

F: Well, it's your position because you represent him.

T: Well, I'm John Barron!

F: You're the publicist. It's normal for me to talk to the publicist. So that's your position.

T: That's his position. Not my position, though!

F: Part of the fun of these lists is that people drop off, people come back on, you know. Our readers understand that the marketplace can be volatile and that fortunes ebb and flow for a variety of reasons and that's why a snapshot of the wealthiest people—

T: Your readers—your readers are going, "What's happening with Trump? What's going on with Trump? What's Trump doing? Trump's on the TV, Trump's showing up on *Donahue*, Trump's everywhere." Listen to me, Trump runs everything, he's all over the place. You know, we just got a property, we're just working on an additional property at the LaGuardia terminal. It's going to be an incredible two-story storage unit—it's going to be incredible, you can store all kinds of cargo, things like that—

F: All right, sir, I don't think my readers are going to be interested in an air cargo storage facility.

T: Are you kidding me? Haven't you ever read *Air Cargo News*? Listen, I don't want to say anything, but I hear that Donald Trump's going to be in the alleyway near Studio 54 tomorrow, trying to get in the back through a door that's been left unlocked.

F: I don't understand.

T: I'm just saying, if a certain *Fortune* reporter wanted to catch Donald Trump having a great time. And see how much money he has. That would be a perfect opportunity.

F: The process for reporting your income for the purposes of our story is well defined. As a publicist, I imagine you already know what it is.

T: Uh . . . I do, but you should tell me.

F: Well, we do a survey of publicly available information in terms of your holdings and tax disclosures, and then we take personal information direct from the source or the source organization to verify everything. We count personal funds, real estate holdings, other—

T: He's got so much real estate!

F: It sounds to me like the company has holdings.

T: He's the holdings. He's the guy who holds it.

F: If the company has the holdings, then Mr. Trump's personal share would be based on the ownership structure of the company—

T: He's the company.

F:—which I believe is split between multiple family members, wives, ex-wives, shareholders—

T: No, no, it all changed today. Trump owns 98, 99, maybe more.

F: Well, fax me over a document to that effect, because that would be a story.

T: *Fax?!*

INTERVIEW: THE TALLEST BUILDING IN NEW YORK

Kelsey: Let's talk about Trump Tower. You tore down the original Bonwit Teller building and built your seventy-five-story tower.

T: Eighty-five. Eighty-five. And first off, yeah, of course we tore it down and built another building. That's how you build, dummy! You stick to golf.

K: I will, sir.

T: Trump Tower is the greatest tower. You can't see a single illustration of New York City without Trump Tower shining and gleaming over the rest. It's the most obvious building! Way more obvious than the Twin Towers. Way more identifiable than the Empire State Building. Or that Freedom Tower, have they blown that up yet? Would anybody care? Our building is beautiful, clear, and crisp. Right next to Tiffany's! And I don't mean my backup daughter.

K: Tell me about building it.

T: We started construction in 1979 and it was a big job, let me tell you, there was a lot of negotiation, lots of union stuff we had to deal with, and you know the unions are tough, and they're not always good. They're always trying to railroad you. Too many regulations, too many slowdowns, shutdowns, so, I did it, I scabbed it. And I didn't care. Cause these electricians, doesn't matter, you get five Mexican guys, they know how to wire a building. Then we noticed the building was too small. So I said, why don't we just cut out ten of the floors and then up the number? Then it went from a seventy-five- to an eighty-five-story building. Then it was just right. And I made sure we imported fine reflective copper metal substitute. I got beautiful near-gold plating. I got imitation marble floor mats to lay over the concrete. It was a dream come true. A lot of work went into that tower, let me tell you. But we had to get the tenants.

K: Businesses or people in the apartments?

T: We got both. We got Tower Records. We love Tower Records and we said, this is a perfect match, business-wise, because this is a tower, and to have a tower in the basement, it was a little joke for everybody. And everyone got it and they all laughed. They all laughed all the time. So much fun. And we got the best people moving into Trump Tower. Bruce Willis. Marla Gibbs. And a bunch of incredible LLCs. I love the LLCs. They're a great family. I love the LLCs, they're all so wonderful. Martha Rae, Miss Dentures herself, lives here. It's incredible. Tony Bennett's cousin. And the Russians helped too. The Russians helped a lot with a lot of properties. They put a lot of money in, and I said, "Yeah, you wanna keep it here, go for it." And they'd never move in, which was great because then you could rent to somebody else and make extra money. I also had my hands in a lot of poker rooms in the 1980s and '90s. And again there's the Russians. These Russian guys were tough and they ran great poker games. I would save a little bit off the top of all the gambling, which was a good deal, but don't tell anyone cause it was illegal. Giuliani's a good friend. He's a good friend. And when we finished it, I said, I went to the top, and I took each of my children, and I dangled them off the roof of the tower. And I held them and I said, "Do you believe in Daddy now? Do you believe in Daddy now? You said I couldn't do it. But I did it!" And then I would drop one of their legs, but I would pick them up and put them back in on the tower roof. And then I'd tell the other ones that they made me do it! So I told Ivanka that Marla made me hang her, and I told Don Jr. that Ivanka made me, and I told Eric that Don Jr. did it, and I told Grimace that all the kids wanted him hung over the tower. But the only sad truth is, I lost my grip on Grimace, and he fell to his death. You can still see the stain in the street. I didn't know they bled red or had human bodies inside them!

Rental Application for Trump Tower

1. Salutation: [] MR.

2. Name: Last, First, Middle

[_____]

[_____] [_____]

3. Race (Enter Code)

OK-White

C-Black

Z-Asian

HMM-White Hispanic

NO-Hispanic (other, non-white)

CHIEF-American Indian

COSBY-Black, one of the good ones

4. Current Address

[_____]

[_____]

[_____]

[_____] [_____]

5. Rent-to-own

~~~~~~~~~~~~~~~~

5.1 Name of Daughter, Mistress, or Awful Son Who Will
Technically Own Property

[_____]

[_____] [_____]

5.2 Intermediate LLC Levels (1-9)

[__]

6. Account Balances

~~~~~~~~~~~~~~~~~~~~~~~~~

6.1 Checking Account

[$ _____.00]

6.2 Savings Account

[$ _____.00]

6.3 Offshore Account

[$ _____.00]

6.4 Mystery Fund

[$ _____.00]

6.5 Mattress Balance

[$ _____.00]

7. Monthly Expenses

~~~~~~~~~~~~~~~~~~~~~

7.1 Alimony

[$ _____.00]

7.2 Settlements

[$ _____.00]

[ ] Fault Admitted Y/N

7.3 Protection

[$ _____.00]

7.4 "Protection"

[$ _____.00]

7.5 Trump Foundation

[$ _____.00]

7.6 Other

[$ _____.00]

8. Income Sources

~~~~~~~~~~~~~~~~~~~

8.1 Rental Property

[$ _____.00]

8.2 Palimony

[$ _____.00]

1.8.2 LABOR

Archivist's Note

They show CNN in my hotel gym and at half the bars in DC when there's no ballgame on. To hear them tell it, the country is in dire straits because of Donald Trump. I wonder how they can even see the country from up in their ivory tower. (President Trump just legalized ivory imports again, but if you think they won't find a way to spin that negatively, I have an elephant to sell you.) If you hadn't guessed, I don't much care for cable news. Before I came to Washington, I used to think there wasn't enough real news to fill a twenty-four-hour cycle. Now that I'm "behind the scenes" I know there is plenty of news; they just manage to get it all wrong! I've seen up close how the media lies. They're blinded by their own feelings of illegitimacy that they project onto the president. My wife, Peg, says she's not sure she would vote for Donald Trump again. But she took his call today, didn't she? Because men like him command respect, even from people who say he turns them off. They know they can't stand in the way of his power, and the power of what he represents. A return to order. Reclaiming the birthright of the Americans who built this country. If the country is falling apart, the pathological weakness that has chained our national spirit is to blame. Weakness has made us vulnerable to the hordes of vermin that would devour us while we sleep. Donald Trump is strong. The people around him are strong because of him. I am strong because I am with them, because I belong. Let the millennials take the best stools at the "trendy" bars on their biracial dates where they drink old-fashioneds under Edison bulbs and complain that white men haven't ever done anything right. They don't see what's coming. They won't be ready. (And neither will CNN!)

INTERVIEW: HOLY MATRI-MONEY

Kelsey: Let's talk about marriage.

Trump: I love weddings. Lots of drunk skirts. Are you married?

K: Yes, you spoke to my wife on the phone yesterday.

T: That's right. Peg. Peggy. I like your wife. I call her sometimes.

K: Right. Well. So, you've been divorced twice.

T: Yes. There were a lot of women.

K: Yes sir.

T: A lot of women.

K: We were saying, you're well known for that, sir.

T: Lotta womenuhh . . . Lotta women uuuuhhhhhhhhhh.

K: Are you all right, sir?

T: A lot of women. God. Just thinking about it!

K: You're soaking wet, sir.

T: Yeah. I get sweaty when I think about all those hot ladies in the '70s I was doing. I used to wait on line at Studio 54 and half the time I would get turned away. So I would go to a little place called Plato's Retreat. It was in the Upper West Side and they had a delicious seafood buffet. And in the basement they had a bunch of mattresses! You could do anybody you wanted. Buck Henry used to hang out there! Buck Henry was there. And let's just say there are a number of stained mattresses somewhere in a museum, incredible history. Anyway, then I met Ivana. And she was, I mean, listen. Could I have done better? Of course I could've. But I knew she had the genes to make a beautiful daughter. I had a dream. A great crow with seven eyes appeared and spoke to me. And it said, "You'll have the most beautiful daughter, and she will be your wife."

K: This is Ivana?

I: Ivana gave me my wife.

K: I'm not sure I understand.

T: It was 1976, give or take. I was at an incredible party and this beautiful woman came in with her friends. And they couldn't get a seat at the restaurant. So I went over to the maître d' cause I knew the guy, and I said, "Listen to me, you gotta get these honeys a table, cause I think I can get with them." So he went over to a table full of the poorest people in the restaurant and said, "Get out of here! Get out of here, you poor garbage, or you'll eat in the street!" They had a busboy chase them away with a mop. So I said to Ivana, "You're coming home with me." And she said, "Absolutely not." And she didn't. And I said, "This is a shrewd woman." Because I would have hit and run, because there was no DNA and the rules were different at the time. But because she said no to me, I said, "Now I'm gonna have you for life!" Just like my presidency. And we got together and it was all wonderful.

We took the jets, we had the caviar, we ate the blinis, we drove everywhere you could drive, we flew everywhere we could fly, and when we couldn't do that, we got on a boat! But we did it. And then I said to her, "Will you be the love of my life and marry me and sign this nondisclosure agreement and various other legal documents so that we can be joined together? So that no one will know what I'm like in private or the fact that I sometimes get rough with people?" And we did. And we did great business together and we have a lot of great memories, we did a Pizza Hut commercial together, and that was a lot of fun. We did a McDonald's—oh no, that was Grimace! That wasn't Ivana.

K: You and Ivana had three children.

T: Ivana was a great mother. I was working on the business—I didn't have time! The kids would play Legos in the office, but mostly I ignored them. She'd take them to the park, she'd take them over here, she'd take them over there, and then she'd bring them in to me and she'd say, "Let me introduce you to your children. This is Ivana, this is Don Jr., this is Eric, and this is Ivanka." And when I looked at my daughter, it was like time stopped. My vision went blurry and everything melted away when I saw her. What a beauty. And I said, "That's my . . . That's me and Ivana combined to make Ivanka? Wow." She got the great genes. Only the best parts. Listen, I'm a good-looking guy, but I can't compete with Ivanka. She'd win a talent show. She'd win the beauty pageant every time. And I'll tell you this: We've done family swimsuit competitions. She always cleans up. And I'm the judge! I make the boys do the swimsuits with bags over their heads so you can't tell the difference. It's like a couple hot pears rolled into the room. But my boys are wonderful, Eric, Don Jr., and Grimace. A lot of people don't know this, but when Eric was born, he was just teeth and gums. We put it in a special tank and grew the rest of the parts from other babies that passed away in the ER that night, you know, caught a case of the pillows. And Don Jr., I remember when I gave him my name, we stood in my office looking out at Central Park and I put my arm around him and said, "Together, we could own this town."

K: So you left Ivana for Marla Maples.

T: Well, this was the time when I was working a lot of hours. It was very busy. I was spending a lot of time out at gala events because as you know I do a lot of charity. And one day I meet this beautiful woman, Marla Maples. And she had just been on Gary Hart's boat. She was with Gary Hart, who was running for president. They were having a big affair, but couldn't do it, because this guy is a politician. And I always beat politicians. So when she broke up with him after the photos surfaced, she ran right into my arms, and she went, "Donald, Donald, you gotta save me." And I said, "Honey, why don't you come sit in my lap in the spinny chair." So we stayed up late that night and let's face it. I did something I wasn't supposed to do. And I don't want to say too much, but I put my little pickle in the jar. And then my friend John Barron called the *New York Post* and said, "Guess what?! Donald Trump's sticking it to someone else! But don't tell anybody, because I'm his publicist!" And then I said, "Isn't Donald the most handsome guy? I mean, all the women are chasing him. You can't get 'em off him!" And it was true, but Marla got pregnant with . . . uh . . . uh . . .

K: Are you looking for something in that pile of papers?

T: My daughter . . . uh . . . uh . . .

K: Are you okay?

T: Tiffany.

K: Tiffany.

T: I made Marla sign an incredible agreement, and the crow came back and said, "Hey, that's pretty brutal what you're doing to Ivana," and I said, "Shut up, crow! Tell me about the new daughter, Tiffany!" And the great crow said, "Well . . . she's sweet." And I said, "Oh great. Wonderful." I went one daughter too far. And Marla turned out to be a real drip. She was nothing like the *Sports Illustrated* version of her that was wet, quiet, and in a bikini. Instead she was dry, loud, and real. All she wanted to do was sit and talk or go on vacations. So with Marla, it was even shorter than with Ivana. We divorced after six years of marriage. One short of the seven-year itch. Always get out before the seven-year itch. Because when that itch happens, it's a very expensive cream to get rid of it. So I pushed Marla off the wagon train, and it was off to Melania. I was at a nightclub to meet a friend and I saw her, and what a beautiful model she was. I thought, what is this, the movie *Mannequin*? Is she gonna become a mannequin at midnight every night? But then I figured out it was more like *Weird Science* or the cartoon movie where he falls in love with a cartoon. It's every guy's dream to use a machine to create a woman and then change her because you can. And we're getting closer to that, it's just a shame Bill Pullman won't be there to see it. So I turned to Melania and said, "Are you the coat check girl?" And she said no. And I said, "Will you marry me?" And a few years later, she did!

Melania. I love women who are named after vowels so when I finish saying their name my mouth can go soft, open, and wet for a kiss. I'm a kissy boy. And here's the thing. I also picked these names because I can't learn a new way to say a woman's name. So I keep them in the ballpark of some sort of "aayahh." And our relationship, and I really believe this, our relationship is based off the fact that our relationship is over. Finally I found the love of my life, a woman who didn't like me before we got married. Nobody likes me. Who could love me? Nobody could love me. I'm too great. Now, the night I met Melania, after I gave her my coat ticket and she walked away, the crow came to me one last time and it said, "Don't have a fifth kid. Whatever you do." And I said, "Shut up, crow, and blow me." And the crow blew me. His sharp beak, it was so hot. And you can make eye contact because there were seven eyes so there was always one to catch. And then I woke up and it was a year later and I was underneath the chocolate fountain and Melania saved me. I almost drowned in the Mar-a-Lago chocolate fountain. You've seen it.

K: Yes.

T: She picked me up and she took me to the bedroom. I knew to put the red sheets on tonight, because I was gonna break my seal. I had stayed a virgin this entire time.

DONALD.ORG

Itinerary: 2013 Miss Universe Moscow

DAY ONE (11/07/2013): NYC->JFK

DEPARTURE

17:00: Toilet time

17:45: White stretch Hummer limo arrives Trump Tower

18:00: DT gets in limo hot tub

18:15: Travel to JFK

18:30: Towel off and remove DT from hot tub

18:45: CALL: DT informs Melania of Russia trip

FLIGHT

22:00: Call time for DECOY STEWARDESS

22:40: In-flight movie: *Finding Nemo*

22:50: Warm towels

23:00: DT sleeps at scary part—DO NOT TURN OFF MOVIE!

04:40: Scheduled turbulence

04:45: DECOY STEWARDESS beverage service

04:55: DECOY STEWARDESS escorts DT to first-class bathroom

05:00: ██████████

05:55: DT watches frozen doodie fly by window

06:15: Warm towels

06:30: *Finding Nemo* 2

Pack up piles of newspapers and take-out containers for shipment.

Don't forget your booties!

07:10: DT enjoys crash position

07:13: Pilot announcement: "We're crashing, we're crashing!"

07:15: Touchdown Moscow

DAY TWO (11/08/2015): MOSCOW

CAR FROM AIRPORT

08:25: Scout potential locations for TRUMP MOSCOW

08:45: Pass by President ███████████ residence, DT makes phone call
to President ███████████

MOSCOW RITZ

10:00: Check in to Moscow Ritz Carlton presidential suite, SPECIAL
HOUSEKEEPING REQUEST: ███████████

10:15: Preliminary team removes all fresh fruit and juices from hotel
room

10:25: Preliminary team delivers ornate basket of candies and meats

10:30: DT checks in to room for private time

10:35: CALL TIME for DECOY MAID (Decoy Stewardess Wig Change—
30min / Wardrobe Provides French Maid Costume)

PAGEANT VENUE INSPECTION

12:25: Gold Oldsmobile "Goldsmobile" with second engine arrives

12:28: Refresh meat basket

12:30: DT arrives in lobby

12:30–12:45: DT Free wander, force strangers into conversation

12:45: DT departs in Goldsmobile to pageant venue

13:15: Swing by President ███████████'s place again, DT leaves
note

EMERGENCY BAG: BK BROILER, SEPT 1986 PLAYBOY CENTERFOLD, HOT WHEELS GARBAGE TRUCK, PURPLE GEODE

SET DRESS / COMMERCIAL FLIGHT AS PRIVATE

TRUMP MUST BELIEVE THIS IS A PRIVATE JET!

13:25: Arrive at Venue Crocus City Hall

14:00: Re-explain concept of loading dock to DT

14:00–14:10: Wait for truck, bait DT w/ BK Broiler

14:30: Appointment with Jeanie Kontrovavic

14:45: Sound check, allow for extra time with DT doing *Police Academy* routine into mic

15:00: Check lights, DT runs from stage to audience trying to see what he looks like up there

18:40: DT personally checks runway for slickness

18:45: Venue toilet time

19:10: Depart venue

DINNER WITH ███████████

19:45: Prep team arrives with ketchup

20:00: Arrive at TGI Fridays Moscow

20:25: Appeteasers

21:00: Tableside Video Conference with President ████████████ attended by ███████████

21:30: Appetizers

21:45: Hamburger mountain

22:00: DECOY WAITRESS offers aperitif (wardrobe provides wig switch for DECOY MAID)

22:10: DT and DECOY WAITRESS toilet time.

22:45: Depart for Ritz

23:00: Arrive at Ritz

23:15: Room service appeteasers

23:30: DT rolled into sleep position

DAY 3 (11/09/2015): PAGEANT DAY

MORNING

05:30: Stroke DT awake from night panics

05:35: Deny trip through mirror

05:40: Toilet time

06:10: Call Ivanka

06:20: Hair application and shaping

07:20: Call Ivanka

07:30: DT open wander, knock on other doors on floor

07:45: Breakfast sandwich cart

07:50: Replica General Lee arrives hotel valet

08:00: Trump departs hotel for pageant

PAGEANT

08:30: Arrive venue. Explain loading dock concept.

08:45: DT greets judges

09:00: DT lingers near contestant dressing room

09:30: DT steps closer to entrance to contestant dressing room

09:45: Taco bar open

09:50: Taco time/DT completes necessary paperwork

10:00: DT lingers near contestant dressing room

10:15: Call Ivanka

10:30: Call Melania re: daily disappointment

10:45: Call Ivanka

11:00: Enter contestant dressing room

11:01: Examine contestants

11:03: Exit contestant dressing room

11:04: Re-enter contestant dressing room

11:05: Toilet time (wardrobe provides change of pants)

11:15: Taco time

11:45: Broadcast feed sound and video check

11:55: DT takes seat between ██████████ and ██████████

12:00: Pageant begins

13:55: Pageant breaks for judging

14:00: DT private meeting with judges outside contestant dressing room

14:05: DT strips ██████████ eligibility, overrides ██████████, names ██████████ winner

14:10: DT barges in to contestant dressing room (wardrobe to provide change of pants)

14:30: Winner announced

14:35: Call to President ██████████

14:45: Conference call with Deutche Bank officers re: account ██████████

15:00: Depart venue

16:00: Arrive Ritz

17:00: Room service dinner

17:30: Call Ivanka

19:30: Schiller leaves

20:00: Entertainment provided by ██████████ arrives

20:15: ██████████, ██████████, ██████████, and ██████████ arrive with ██████████ for "Operation Piss Party"

21:30: Housekeeping request for new linens, pillows, after ██████████

22:00: Taco time

23:00: Roll DT into sleeping position

DAY FOUR (11/10/2015)

08:00: DT transported sleeping to cargo plane

09:00: Failsafe tranquilizer administered

09:30: DT impersonator calls Melania

10:00: Wheels up, cargo plane returns to LaGuardia Marine Air
   Terminal
10:30: DT revived, admires WPA mural
11:00: Toilet time

THE CAMPAIGN

Trump's Diary: White House Correspondent's Dinner 2011

I walked the red carpet from my limousine. With all the real press attending the dinner, the photographers on the red carpet were the lowest of the low. I was happy to give them a little star power. An old woman asking for autographs. Her name was **Helen Thomas**. Blogger boys with their crumpled headshots. And I was greeted at the door by **Wolf Blitzer**, who was staring confusedly at the grandfather clock. His beard was stinky with mustard from the veal sausage he enjoys before every public appearance. There were so many beautiful women greeting me at the door. Obviously DC had turned out its five top tens. There's no decent ass in this city, just a bunch of over-the-hill dye jobs with nothing better to do than ask you questions all the time. I sat down at my table, an unattractive purple cloth covered it. Mauve. Boring. And the cutlery was standard caterer-issued cutlery. I know that better than anyone else. We do a lot of catering jobs at the Trump Tower. And they're always signature bone china. Only the finest. From China! China from China. I looked to my left and who would be sitting at my table but none other than **Andrea Mitchell**. Word around town is that her husband asks her to dress up as Ayn Rand or he can't get a stiff beam in his building. And there was **Phil Donahue**, a man, a great man, and such a great interviewer, whose interview with me is so timeless that it is part of my postcoital ritual.

ITEM: Steve Bannon was seen exiting Spirit Walking, currently the hottest occult bookstore in DC. Steve took some time to chat with a Wiccan Masseuse while browsing the dollar book bucket.

Was that a little boy serving cocktails? No, it was just **Rachel Maddow** bringing drinks to her table. But boy oh boy. Does she look like the smoothest little boy you'd have working in your backyard. I was lucky enough to see that human barrel of fermented cheese, **Sean Hannity**, lumbering up to me. Sean's a tough guy. He's got a haircut like a 1920s oil baron. He's got the attitude to match. But he's great on the phone, he loves to chat, which is a lost art. Sean asked me how my night was going. I said, "Fantastic! I'm here for food, laughs, and fun." Finally I made it to the table, even if it was to watch that caramel impostor stand up at the podium. The truth was, I was with my peers.

ITEM: Who's that buying a box of Just for Young Men Who Want to Look Distinguished? at the CVS? David Gregory's roots are showing!

I didn't know who **Seth Meyers** was. I never watched that show. But I knew who Michael Myers was, because he was very frightening in my favorite Halloween movie, *Wayne's World*. Seth Meyers was first up to the podium, and boy was this guy boring. The thing guys like him don't get is that when they send me up, it makes people who like me like me even more. By the time he finished with his jokes I wasn't paying attention.

Megyn Kelly was looking beautiful that night. I would love to get with her. I could catch a shoulder and the back of an ear but it wasn't gonna do it for me.

ITEM: It's true! legendary newsman Howard Fineman has two copies of every postpresidential election *Newsweek*. One has the actual winner on the cover and the other is the cover if the other candidate had won, so his house is useless for helping a time traveler get a handle on his situation.

With no one to seduce or grab or berate, I started sinking inside myself. But then suddenly the clouds opened up and I became the topic of conversation again. But it wasn't the funny guy talking. I knew this voice. I could hear him saying my name, but there was a tugging sensation inside me that kept pulling me down. I never sweated so much in my life! Someone must have changed the lights, because I could only see straight forward in front of me. And in red! It was a wild lighting design they did. Totally immersive performance. Because I felt sick. It must have been the quail egg appetizer. But suddenly all I could see were mouths moving as a slow hum was building in my head. A ringing in my ears and my own heart beat rattling in my chest. I couldn't catch my breath! Was I having a heart attack? No, I'm too healthy for that! But something was going on. Something was opening inside of me. It felt like poison in my stomach. Or maybe a fire in my belly. I'm not sure. But every time that big fake opened his mouth and said my name, I felt my blood rise. I said to myself, "I gotta get rid of this guy." I gotta do it somehow. The birth certificate thing wasn't working, so maybe I had to take him out.

I heard my name repeated over and over again, an awful and inappropriate assault on my character—which is totally incredible—as I heard this false president sputtering such lies, I felt something crack open in my head. It was as if light was crowding around my eyes. My stomach turned. The sour-smelling sweat ran down my back. I've had this feeling before. This is the same feeling when Mother used to speak to me or I used to get called out in class for not doing my homework. And I know when I feel this feeling, I know there's only one thing to do: Whatever I think of in that moment, without thinking twice, do it as hard as possible. And this time, it was run for president.

INTERVIEW: THIS AMERICAN CARNAGE STARTS NOW

Kelsey: You descending down the escalator at Trump Tower to announce your candidacy has become an iconic moment.

Trump: It's a great moment.

K: Did you know when you were coming down that escalator that you were about to change the course of history?

T: I didn't know. I had no idea. I didn't know what I was doing. In fact, I didn't know why I was on that escalator. Melania said to me, "Let's go down to the lobby for a second." And I said, "Let's go down to the lobby, let's go down to the lobby, let's go down to the lobby and buy a Diet Coke at the newsstand!" It's a little joke I do for her every day. She loves it so much. She always says, "What is that? What is that?" And I say, "Well, in old movies, they'd always have a little song in the movie theater." And she says, "Oh, Donald, I'm bored," and then she goes to the other room. So it was a total surprise. It was like a surprise party, for me!

And so I got to the podium, and I said, you know what, I'm going to run for president. Because there's already a podium here. And I announced. Listen, it was the first time I had ever tried to run for president recently. We'd been focus testing slogans and buying data and we had all the odds against us. We were a small operation. I mean, I got a lot of money, but not like the Super PACS. Not like the Bushes, I mean Bush, this guy had $418 million to start out! I had nothing. So we thought we'd give it our best shot, but we knew the people were on our side. And we had real issues to fix. Nobody was talking about immigration before me. Nobody was talking about immigration. Nobody was talking about the wall. Nobody was talking about these things. So we took the escalator. The escalator roll that was heard around the world. Sort of a low hum. So I went down, and I gave my speech, and then I went upstairs, and then next thing I knew I was president of the United States. When was the inauguration, like a week later?

K: No sir, it was almost two years.

T: Okay, well. We had a lot of work to do, there were a lot of big guys in there. Seventeen. Seventeen of the best. The best Republican candidates. Some of the best. You had Chris Christie, big fat guy, big tub, gotta have one of those. Gotta have a big fat guy. Every great comedy does. And you had the little guy, Rand Paul, who was the old lady who could rap. Jeb Bush. I thought Jeb was gonna be way tougher. He was boring! Jeb had nothing to do. He was the Terri Schaivo of candidates. You know who I liked, and I'll tell you this: Ted Cruz, total slimeball. But that guy can fight. He's a real rat. So anyway, that was how the introduction began.

K: They said that both you and Hillary Clinton had a lot in common—

T: Crooked Hillary.

K: Because you both— **T:** Say it!

K: Crooked Hillary.

T: There you go.

K: Because you both spent a lot of time, more than any other candidates in history, you returned home to sleep in your own bed almost every night.

T: That's right. Only my bed. My bed is incredible. It's adjustable. It's Posturpedic and Craftmatic and Jurassic all the wonderful-ic's that we all know. And it has a remote that can tip itself up. And it's incredible because you can sit in the bed, eat TV-tray dinner, watch the news, watch yourself on the news, and—I gotta say—I like my own bed. Even Melania doesn't sleep in that bed! I sleep in my own bed. It's the prototype for the Trump Hotel Mattress, but don't tell Pruitt, he still has keys to the White House. So I would always go home. I don't like staying in other hotels because you don't know the cameras, the people who are seeing you and watching you in the dirty beds.

K: You have a lot of turnover on your campaign, between Cory Lewandowski and Paul Manafort and Carter Page and all the people who came on board to your campaign and—

T: Crooks. All crooks. And they had nothing to do with the campaign. They had very little to do with the campaign, okay? I mean, Carter Page was basically sitting around there doing nothing. And then you had, who's the other guy? See, I don't even know the guy! None of them worked there. They all got tied up in this whole Russia thing, they got tied up from the beginning, which is why none of them worked there! They never worked there because they were already with Russia, and Russia was with Russia, and I didn't know them, they didn't work for me. Manafort, that guy did the convention and the Ukrainian platform and that was it! He was basically a big party planner! That guy knows nothing. Nobody knows anything except the people currently working for me, until they also resign or get indicted and then I never worked with them.

Nobody who was talking to Russia was on my campaign. So if somebody was on my campaign and it seemed like they were talking to Russia, they just weren't on my campaign. Eric wasn't there. No one was there who talked to Russia. If you talked to Russia you were ignored, like a ghost! The Russians would come in for a meeting, they would sit down, no one would be in the room, and they'd leave. Nobody there. They just sat in the room, they talked into the air, and left. And that's how it worked. Through the whole campaign. And they were just talking about adoptions anyway which is babies, and we all know that.

K: Was winning the presidency the hardest thing you've ever done?

T: It was an incredible victory. We won the electoral college by a huge margin, it was the biggest margin since they invented the notepad. But I'll tell you, it was tough. Iowa? Tough place. Ted Cruz won first, I came in second. And in every state, I'd see the coal miners, and they'd say, "Where's the mine?" And I'd say, "I promise you I'm gonna dig a mine, I'm gonna find the caves, we're gonna get you back in the caves." And here's why Iowa went for Ted, okay, stupid Iowa, they don't have caves! No coal. They only have corn. You dig underground, it's just more corn. And let me tell you something, there's no such thing as clean corn technology, cause I've looked in the toilet and there's nothing clean about that. And it's not a fossil fuel! A fossil fuel would be taking the dinosaur and burning it in a furnace, which is a great opportunity.

My base! You know, some people would say I was so good at finding my base that I'm the Ace of Base. Cause I saw the signs. And there were so many signs. This base is troubled. They wanna work. They're the forgotten men and forgotten women of this country. The people who are discriminated against just because they're white. Just because they're white. Just because they're poor and they don't have anything and they don't have anything to piss in. And the worst thing about the forgotten men and the forgotten women is that they forgot each other! Nobody's dating! Everything's online now and there's no forgotten men or forgotten women dating website. But the truth is that these people didn't forget one thing: their heritage. And the truth is that we need it. And listen, you wanna walk around with a tiki torch? Maybe you're going to a barbecue. That's not my business. David Duke, brilliant guy, tough guy, but I disavow. I disavow. *Daily Stormer*? I read it all the time, and I disavow it.

K: Just back to all the turnover on your campaign. The NSA was monitoring Carter Page and Mike Flynn because they thought they were participating in what was essentially an espionage operation against the United States.

T: No, excuse me, excuse me, the dossier's totally fake. There's no collusion. There's no collusion. The dossier was fake. Like I'm gonna make a peepee on somebody? I'm gonna let someone peepee on my bed? Are you crazy? I'm not gonna let someone peepee on my bed. They peepee in a bucket and dump it on me on the porch. Why don't you try it, see what happens, I won't touch you.

K: I'm not going to.

T: Do it.

K: I'm not going to try.

T: Okay, you have another question. Ask me ask me ask me.

K: Okay. So. You really came alive at your rallies. Your base loved the rallies. What do you think it is about your rallies that allows you to connect so directly with people?

T: I'm the same as them. I'm just a guy who's up there talking, and they're all talking to me. And we have a good time, we have free T-shirts, we have a wet T-shirt contest in the back. We connect because we speak the same language. They hate a lot of things, and I hate a lot of things. And we hate those things together. And we like publicly beating up black people and gay people in a large arena, or at least thinking about it and pantomiming a little bit! And if any of them stopped paying attention I'd just start talking about the wall. Or I'd say Iran's real dangerous and we might get nuked. And I used to spend a lot of time doing prop work with my belt and whether Ben Carson could get stabbed. Boy, that was some great material. The truth is, we had so much fun, we did it all the time, and we did it right. And, at the end of the day, when we'd leave there'd be a good old-fashioned riot! I remember one time, some guy tried to jump up on the stage, and I got scared, and I turned and ran around like a cuckoo chicken. Then they said, "You're fine, you're fine," so I continued giving the speech and I was sweating the entire time. Cause I thought that guy was gonna get me! But he didn't. And it's pretty amazing folks, that nobody even really tried. Hillary, you go to her rallies, and it's like, "Oh, ooh, can I have some tea, Grandma?" Boring! It was like a bridge party, and all the ladies were so stupid. There's a reason there's a glass ceiling, and it's so you can look up skirts. Let me ask you something. Let me ask you something. You want a drink? You like whiskey?

K: I wouldn't turn down a little—

T: Good, good, here, I got you one. They tell me it's good stuff, I got it from Canada, they need strong stuff up there because they're so shy. This good? You want a double? This is good. Now I've got a question for you.

K: Okay.

T: Here's a scenario, writer guy. How's your drink, is it good?

K: Yes sir.

T: Good. So here's a scenario. Okay. Door opens, Sixteen-year-old comes into the room. One of my pageant girls. Universal girl, universal. Beautiful, so beautiful.

K: Yes sir.

T: Okay. She's so pretty. And she's like looking at you, and she's like—What's your name again?

K: Kelsey.

T: She's like, "Ooooh, Kelsey, I know I'm only sixteen, but I'm a woman!" And—

K: Sir, I'm reminding you we're on the record.

T: That's fine, and then—

K: I'd like to take you off the record for this.

T: No, do not take me off the record.

K: I'd really like to take you off the record.

T: And then she says to you, she says, "You can do whatever you want with me, and your wife will never know. You can have the next two hours with me. And I'll be a pleasure machine."

K: No. Sir, I'd like to stop this conversation—

T: And right before you kiss her she goes, "And by the way, I'm your daughter from the future, but I came back in time." Would you do her?

K: No sir.

T: Would you, really?

K: I wouldn't even before the time travel.

T: But she's come back from the future, so she's not even real yet! Look, I'd do it. And so would you. Here. You want another drink?

K: This is good stuff.

T: Here, enjoy. We're done working tonight. This is our time. Let's have some fun. You wanna go out?

K: I guess I'd go out for one.

T: For one. Let's go out for one. You mind if it's a strip club? You mind if there's girls?

K: I don't mind.

T: I hear you. There will be girls. I know a place, there's girls and, you know, it's no problem if you want to. They want you to. You're coming in with the president, you know. I used to get this kind of thing going in New York, and I gotta say it's even crazier down here, the things people get up to. You want to go?

K: I'll check it out.

T: Girls. College girls. You want that? You want to get some?

K: Yeah. Yeah, okay. Let's go.

T: Hear that? Hear that, sweetie?

Peg Nelson: Jesus Christ, Kelsey.

T: Now you've got no excuse.

ITINERARY: CAMPAIGN RALLY, 2016

16:00: Minorities and protesters arrive at venue, rehearse

17:00: Trump arrives venue

17:15: Trump screams "shithole!" at map of town

17:30: Inspect Diet Coke catheter

17:45: Spin Chant Wheel: Options: "Lock Her Up" "Build the Wall" "Little Marco Run" (PROP: water cup) "YMCA"

18:00: Send Eric and Don Jr. to collect merchandise money, remind Eric to use the designated money bucket

18:30: Dinner from local Dollar Menu

19:00: Review speech, free wander

PROTESTER HAS OWN H/MU TEAM

19:05: Trash speech, wing it

19:15: Flynn WARMS UP CROWD

19:30: Trump to stage

19:50: Protester

20:00: Ambulance and protestor signs timesheet

21:30: Toilet time

22:15: Call Ivanka

22:30: Campaign town car to regional airport via Taco Bell

23:15: Wheels up to Teterboro

23:30: Deviation to Cayman Islands airstrip, coordinate with Alexi ███████ for arrival and transfer ████████ into cargo hold

---

TRANSCRIPT: DEBATE PREPARATION

Roger Ailes: You have to prepare.

Trump: Roger, I'm doing so incredible. These debates are so easy, they're totally easy. Jesus, slow down with the toast! How much toast do you need? You got bacon, and you got a side of sausage. It's too much.

R: Donald, you have to prepare. You have an entire apparatus you can take advantage of. We have our shows, we have the network, we have talk radio, we have the Internet. Everybody is going to line up behind you, you just have to decide what you're going to say and you have to say it. And you have to get out ahead of this stuff, Donald. You have to get out ahead of it. You have to prepare.

T: Is that a fourth egg under your potatoes?

R: You can't wing it. You want to hit her. You want to hit her on the affairs.

T: Oh, I wanna hit her.

R: You wanna hit her on the affairs. Bill's affairs.

T: Slick Willy. That guy. He had that black baby, right?

R: It's hard to say.

T: I think he did. I bet we can find the black baby. Let's bring a black baby to the debate! He can sit in the front row and then we'll kick him out.

R: I'm here to help, whatever you need.

T: Did you really make all those moves on those girls? I mean how many are we talking? How many?

R: I get around. My wife doesn't mind. My wife doesn't mind a little extracurricular . . .

(laughs) (hacking cough)

T: Yeah, yeah yeah, yeah! My wife doesn't mind either! Yeah, that's right, my wife doesn't mind either. Just don't tell her. Just don't tell her anything, okay? What's happening, are you choking? Are you breathing? Take it slow. Work it down, I can see the lump in your throat! How much sausage did you put in your mouth? I'm taking advice from a guy who's eating meat like a Muppet? Roger, you don't look so good, you know that? You're getting all gray.

R: What can I do, can we get Kellyanne in? Kellyanne's here, Kellyanne's ready to prep.

Kellyanne Conway: I'm here, sir.

T: Smartest girl in the room.

KC: I'm prepared to play Hillary, sir, and say some of the uncomfortable, awful, unfair things she might say to you.

T: Are you loyal to me, or you still like Ted Cruz? Be honest.

KC: Nobody likes Ted Cruz.

T: That's right. See Roger over here? Look at that. Look at his little hands.

R: Hi, sweetie.

T: See those little hands?

R: Look at you.

T: Those hands have been in more honeypots than you can imagine.

R: Look at you, come over here, you wanna sit in my lap while I finish my sausage?

T: Roger, that's enough! Not here, Roger. Kellyanne's respectable. What is this, a Bob Guccione movie on Cinemax? Guccione was one of the greats. If you can get Guccione on the phone, I'll tell you, that guy's got stories. He'd beat the pants off of you! You're shooting fish in a barrel over at Fox, right? All those honeys doing the news? I mean, you must be losing your mind. You must be losing your mind!

R: Hey, it's good to be the boss, huh?

(Ailes hacks violently)

T: Oh my god. Pick that up off the floor. It's half-chewed.

R: That's a lump.

T: That's not your breakfast? The hell is that? What the hell is that, then?

R: All right, all right.

T: No, no. Don't "all right all right" me, Roger. If you just spat up something that looks like meat, but that's not meat you ate, what is that?!

R: Listen. I got my own problems over at Fox. That's why I'm working on your campaign. I'm not there much longer, I'm on my way out. The writing's on the wall. What I think we should do—

T: It's unbelievable. It's so unfair.

R: You make the best showing you can in this campaign, and if you win, you're the president of the United States.

T: Oh no! I don't want that! We're supposed to make it look good, but not good enough.

R: If you lose, we start our own network, we buy out TruTV or IFC or Spike. You win, you're the president. Now, hold on, it wouldn't be that bad.

T: No! No!

R: Don't worry, you're going to lose. You'll lose and we'll buy our own cable network where anything goes as far as the staff is concerned and we cry foul for eight years.

T: Let me tell you something, Kellyanne. Do you know this? Roger Ailes is the only guy I've ever met who fingered four women at the same time. Unbelievable.

KC: Sir, I'm—

T: Tell the story. Roger, tell the story.

KC: Mr. President . . .

T: What? You like to flirt. We flirt. You can flirt with Roger.

KC: Sir, you're a powerful, charismatic man.

T: Thank you!

KC: This guy is a pig from hell.

T: Roger, wake up. Roger! Wake up!

(Ailes chokes himself awake)

T: What's that?! Now that's definitely not sausage. And it's not bread either!

R: Get over here, Kellyanne.

KC: Sir, sir, please.

T: Get over there, Kellyanne. Get over there. Get over there.

K: Oh my god.

T: It wasn't that bad, it wasn't that bad. I watched, it wasn't that bad. All right, Kellyanne, all right, okay great, time for you to go.

KC: But I was going to play Hillary Clinton. That's why I'm here.

T: Well, I thought you'd want to leave after what happened.

KC: He just grabbed my thigh and shuddered for thirty seconds. It was embarrassing. And now he's passed out.

T: Wait, put a mirror under his face and see if he's alive. No, get closer, Kellyanne! You can't get breath from there, get closer!

KC: He's alive. He's still chewing on a little piece of pork roll.

T: Here's the problem, Kellyanne. Kellyanne, here's the scary thing. We didn't order pork roll. There's no pork roll anywhere in this building. So where'd that pork roll come from?

KC: Maryland, sir?

T: What?! That doesn't answer the question. I think Roger's producing his own pork roll out of his body.

KC: Sir, we really have to prepare.

T: I *am* preparing! What if they ask about this?

KC: They're not going to, sir. The debate is tomorrow.

T: Roger is a genetically altered creature who produces pork products. That's the only answer. You know, I noticed his tongue looks larger and more black today. You think there's something wrong with him? Roger! Roger!

(Ailes snorts awake)

T: Roger, you've done a lot of conquesting. Tell me your best one.

R: Well, I remember, there was one honey, there was a honey that was a field reporter, we'd send her out for some man-on-the-street work—

T: Working girl.

R: She filled in for Greta van Susteren a few nights. And she was moving up in the business, so I invited her up to my office. And I told her if she wanted to move up at the network, she knew what to do. So I leaned back in my chair, I put my hands up behind my head, and she quit.

T: What?! Wow!

R: That's right! I said, "You know what to do," and she says, "I'm tendering my resignation."

T: And then what'd she do, did she blow you?

R: No, she sued us, and she won.

T: Whoa.

R: You know, Bill O'Reilly told me this story. He had this beautiful producer that worked for him.

T: I know the one.

R: And they'd travel together, they'd stay at hotels. And he'd always make sure he had the hotel room booked next door to this honey.

T: I know this trick. Incredible trick.

R: And he said one night they'd been down at the hotel bar at the Ramada, and Bill O. bought her a few extra drinks, and he walked her back up to her room.

T: But she took them, right? She took 'em! She took 'em.

R: That's right.

T: She took them. She took them. She took the drinks. She took the drinks. She took the drinks. She took the drinks. So then what happened?

R: They got up to her room and she said goodnight and shut the door. But Bill was in the room next door hitting the mini bar, so after an hour or so he went tap tap tap on the little door between the two hotel rooms.

T: And she was ready.

R: No.

T: What do you mean?!

R: No! She screamed and then called one of the other producers, who was a guy. He switched rooms with her, and then she quit!

T: What?!

R: And then she sued us and won!

T: Whoa, that's hot. Let me tell you a great story. This is gonna top everything else. So, we were doing Miss Universe, and I was also working on *The Apprentice* at the time. And I had to fly to go to where the Miss Universe was being held out there, which was in Georgia or wherever it was. Somewhere. But I had to be on set at *The Apprentice*. And there was this little thing. She was a little dainty, little dainty girl. And she reminded me so much of my daughter. So beautiful. And one day we had to go fly same day, in the jet, as you know, from the set to go check out the venue for the pageant. And this little honey, she was a PA.

R: She worked for you?

T: She worked for me.

R: Nice!

T: Everybody works for me. Everybody works for me, Roger. High five.

R: I can't.

T: High five.

R: I can't!

T: Just push your little thing into my hand.

R: I can't!

T: That's good enough. And so that morning I ate extra pork sausage like you but I also had salted butter on my toast and I had two chocolate donuts and I had an extra-salty breakfast burrito. And I get on the plane and Roger, she's so beautiful. She gets out of the crowd and sits across from me and I say, "This is it." We're in the air for two hours, and I know I'm getting some real action. Well, as the plane takes off, I don't know if it was the pressure or the fact that I hadn't had any water in days, but I started pitching forward and losing my vision and getting dizzy. But what happened when I fell forward? I fell right into the lap of this beautiful girl. And I tried to start rooting around, but then I was shaking and drooling and she was crying! And boy was she crying. No one makes a girl cry the way I do, you know what I mean? The right way. Well, next thing you know, I'm in a hospital in Georgia. And there's some country doctor guy, you know, some guy with a hayseed, might as well have a hayseed in his mouth, and he says to me, "You had too much salt in your blood, you have too much salt." And I said, "Where's the girl?" And they said, "The woman on the plane?" And I said, "Yeah." And they said, "She's right here." And I said, "I have so much salt in my blood because of all the backup in my balls." And everyone got real quiet in the room. And then the PA said, "I quit!" And the doctor quit with her. And now they're married. Can you imagine that? Anyway, one of the greats. So how are we on the debate prep?

R: Can I have another one of these?

T: Another breakfast? Are you crazy? Roger, one of your eyes is filled with blood. Now tell me honestly, it's just us here. Kellyanne doesn't count. How long does it take for you to pull your penis out from all of your thigh and stomach fat?

R: It's a process of elimination.

T: Mine's like origami. I gotta fold it up. I basically make a crane, and then I can have my peepee. When I meet Xi Jinping, I'm gonna say, "Jin, thank you. Thank you for origami, for without it, I wouldn't get to have fun with my wife, Melania."

KC: Sir?

T: What, Kellyanne?!

KC: I dressed as Hillary Clinton today, and I memorized questions that Hillary Clinton would ask. I want to help you, sir.

T: Fine, let's do questions.

KC: Why would the American people elect a businessman who's gone bankrupt eight times.

T: Wrong. First off, why would Hillary ask me a question? She doesn't run the debate. Trick question. Right, Kellyanne?

KC: No, she'll ask you some questions.

T: She will?

KC: Yes, she'll have the opportunity to challenge you on a few points.

T: Okay . . . uh . . . they'll trust me because I'm not YOU, you witch! What do you think of that?

KC: Pretty good. That'll do it.

T: Gimme another one. Gimme another one. Roger, watch this. Wake up! Roger!

(Ailes moans)

T: Check this out, Roger. Go, Kellyanne. By the way that's not Hillary, it's Kellyanne.

R: I know.

T: Oh, you did? I was trying to play it coy. I just kept pretending to call her Kellyanne cause I thought it was Hillary! That's why I was so cold to you. Sorry, Kellyanne!

KC: This campaign is not a reality show. We need someone with experience in government, not someone with experience on reality TV.

T: If this was a reality show, let me tell you, Geraldo would be mopping the floor with your sorry saggy ass.

KC: Pretty good.

R: Pretty good.

T: Right, Roger? I can do these all day. Gimme another one. Shut up!

KC: There are a lot of questions about your campaign's relationship with the Russian government.

T: Who cares about Russia.

KC: No one's going to want to elect a Russian puppet.

T: Puppet? Who's the puppet? Where's the puppet? Where's the puppet?

KC: You're the puppet.

T: I'm the puppet? No. No puppet. No puppet. No puppet. You're the puppet.

R: Great!

T: You like that one? I'm definitely gonna do that one. Now, where's the puppet?

R: Right here, sir.

T: Wow! Look at that! He's got a little top hat. Is that a bunny? Hi, how are you? Well, Mr. Bunny, nice to talk to you! Why aren't you talking? Are you sad? It's pretty sad. Why's the puppet always leaning forward and never standing straight up? Is he scared? Roger? Roger? Roger?

Archivist's Note

Our interview today was postponed, and not because I woke up in the bathtub of my hotel room with a bruise on my neck (even though I did). I arrived at the West Wing at the usual time, but something was different. John Kelly brought me a cup of coffee, Kellyanne Conway asked me my favorite brand of golf club even though I'm sure she doesn't play. Stephen Miller silently offered me half of his runny breakfast sandwich. Nobody told me where the president was, which was unusual since ten a.m. was usually when he would call down to a subordinate's office and insist that he'd been working hard for hours and order them to announce out loud that they were proud of him. I sat for half an hour listening to the staff complain about their dating lives until the door to the Oval Office finally opened, and to my shock there was the president on the couch in his bathrobe sitting next to my wife, Peg.

I felt the heat shoot up my spine into my neck. If I hadn't already thrown up that morning, I might have vomited all over the most famous office in the world. We hadn't talked in days because this was happening? My head spun with jealousy and rage. How dare she. She was jealous of me for being close to him. Like they're all jealous. The liberals, the Mexicans, the crybaby college students, the women on the news. They want to stop us from our work because they know they don't measure up. I never thought my wife, Peg, would join their numbers. But she had. On her high horse after she'd overheard some boys-will-be-boys on the phone. What men do! I don't blame Trump. Trump's appetites are not for me to question. It was Peg who decided to use her weapon to punish me. But it wasn't going to turn out the way she wanted. If she was trying to separate me from my president, she had miscalculated. The cause I was now a part of was greater than her. The bond I had with this great man was stronger than any man could have with a woman. But if she was trying to get my attention, she had it. The world went black. The next thing I knew I was in a broom closet with Rob Porter, who cracked open a beer and told me that nobody saw anything. Kelly would take care of it. An hour later I went back into the oval office. The president was behind that great oak desk. He smiled at me.

THE PRESIDENCY

General Kelly's Presentation of a Proper Presidential Personage

As a general, protocol is of the utmost importance. But as a gentleman, it is most vital that one comports himself with the manners befitting a member of the noblest class. It is with great excitement and humility that I present you with these pages in which you shall find a collection of axioms and customs which, if properly applied, shall ease the comfort of your-self and your peers both high and low in all affairs you may participate in as president of these United States.

- Watch not the muted television when receiving a visitor to your office or bed chamber.
- Leer not at the interns who enter one's Oval Office, for they are only teenagers.
- Crying out in rage from one's bedchamber is not appropriate at any time of night.
- A president shall refrain from suggesting that watching his chief of staff engaged in a marriage embrace would somehow improve the marriage observed.

- A president shall pay attention to his nuclear codes and shall not place them atop his dining table.
- A president shall take care that White House tablecloths and drapes are not used as napkins nor handkerchiefs.
- No matter the station of the person, it is never appropriate to refer to anyone as "That Brown One."
- Keep in mind that bawdy limericks do not translate to Asian languages.
- Lock not the door while one is bathroom tweeting.
- One's bits and pieces should not be showing while wandering the hallway in an open robe. They are for private only, for a wife, or a mistress. A president shall close his robe while wandering, even when in the private quarters of the White House, but especially in the public areas and gardens.
- Dump not five times a day, but preserve one's bowel for a healthy two movements. One in the morning, and one in the evening.
- Never shake a man or woman's hand so violently that they look around in curious disgust.
- A president shall always take his McDonald's wrappers and place them in the bin beside the bed.
- There is no such game as Find the Nuggets in the Toilet.
- A president shall never tell another man's wife that she should wash her hair more.
- If a man's wife is listening on speakerphone while a president sees fit to invite her husband to solicit prostitutes

with him, make sure the volume is turned to an appropriate level, so that if she chooseth to scream or yell, the intensity of her voice will be translated by the medium.

- When leering at girls between the ages of thirteen and seventeen, a president shall only look at a quarter angle, and always must have a newspaper promptly placed on his lap.

- When calling for a nuclear strike, use a medium to low tone, and recognize that most likely the strike will not happen. It is polite for a president to express his anger, but remember the severity of such an act. Also, the nuclear football may not be used as a Starbucks gift card no matter how many times they may be scanned.

- It is inappropriate for a father to ask his daughter to sit on his lap during trade negotiations.

- When one is speaking to another leader, do not engage in raising of the hand and demonstrating the thumbs-up throughout the conversation.

- A president in a meeting with another diplomat will shake hands firmly and make eye contact and not raise his hand as if to strike him.

- A president shall not use the situation room to rendezvous with pornography actresses of a certain age.

- Throw not candies at female heads of state, nor refer to them as Bowl Cut or Dumptruck.

- A president should always remember to redact certain parts of the Kennedy assassination documents, no matter how intriguing they might be, but he must also never promise to release documents from the Kennedy assassination and then fail to do so.

- A president should reconsider hiring his son-in-law, who has ties to organized crime, as an adviser on a revolving temporary top secret clearance.
- A president shall refrain from referring to his chief of staff as Nancy Pants, or Sillyface, or Miss Frenchie.
- Woe to he who drips in pleasure, for onanistic stains are most unappealing on a White House sofa.
- A president shall purport to maintain a minimally civil relationship with his wife.
- Members of the press should only ask the president pleasing questions about his wall and other things that will bring him delight.
- The staff of the president shall remind the general population that the president does not make waste, but instead has a pure processing system without any holes to evacuate.
- A president would mind himself to apply his Polident liberally to his top bridge before giving speeches.
- A president should spend every day reading the letters of learned men and not depend too slavishly on favored words like "tremendous," "incredible," "believes," and "babies."
- A president shall refrain from curtsying when a subordinate says something flattering to him.

- A president shall take his hair and fold it at six right angles every morning, each one overlapping and folding atop the other. Then he shall apply liberally hair spray to set the hair in a proper position. Once complete, he shall rub cream on the back of his head, which shall be made of gluteal meat so placed on the back of his head such that the lower back of his head might be placed on his head's top.
- A president shall avail himself of a yearly prostate exam.
- The president and his advisers shall bear in mind that there is no president of Taiwan.
- A president shall not make an imitation of a foreign visitor's accent or demeanor as soon as they depart, no matter how silly their voice or comportment.
- He who wishes to serve at the White House but is unable to maintain peaceful relations in his marriage shall purchase a heavy skin cream of appropriate coloring to keep private his wife's eye bruises, or at least a bag of potatoes or oranges. He shall also encourage his abused wife to speak her accusations publicly before the FBI background process has begun in order to save face for his president's chief of staff.

Archivist's Note

I'd ignored my wife Peg's calls until my Android battery ran out. I took the long way back to the Hilton Garden via my favorite liquor store. I got a bottle of something (I remember it being brown, but maybe that was the bag I was half in) and took a ride on the Metro. I always liked trains. The platform was full of thugs. The nation's capital, the trains, the infrastructure; who built that? People like them or people like me? Maybe one of them will throw me on the tracks. It would look like a mugging gone wrong. The president of the United States would tweet about it and make sure these kids would spend the rest of their lives in jail. I wondered what picture of me they'll use on the news next to their high school graduation photos. Maybe the one of me and Peg in St. George's with the little umbrellas. I stood by the edge of the platform and stared. The breeze from the train knocked me off balance and I puked on a bench. The thugs asked me if I was okay. I stumbled onto the train and sat down. I woke up on my feet on the sidewalk near a billiards hall next to a Laundromat. It was full of illegals smoking and dancing and laughing. On a Wednesday night! Who's paying for you to enjoy yourselves? I asked two women sitting out front, one pregnant. I said, How do you stand up with that anchor baby? A salt and pepper guy with a mustache in a gas station uniform told me to fuck off, so I told him to go back to Mexico, I can get into any golf course in the world because that's who I am, and I yelled the president's name until my throat was hoarse. I went looking for the bus and a trans woman (hooray!) took my fifty dollars and told me to catch a cab by the overpass. The cabbie was Korean and I asked him what he thought of the president saving his sorry-ass country. He told me that I didn't have enough money and that I was lucky that girl had let me keep my wallet, so we went to the 7-Eleven, where a guy told me that he was actually a Sikh and that I needed to leave. The woman at the front desk of Hilton Garden Inn wouldn't let me kiss her, so I went upstairs to write a TripAdvisor review. Here are some calls the president made.

BIRTH OF A STATESMAN

CALL: THE INTERNATIONAL SPACE STATION

Trump: Hello? Space?

Peggy Whitson: Hello, Mr. President. It's an honor to speak with you.

T: Miss Peggy Whitson.

P: I'm married and a doctor.

T: Up in the sky. Far above the earth. I'm calling to congratulate you for your space time.

P: Yes sir. I reached a milestone of being the longest person—the longest American in space.

T: How long are you? I didn't know this.

P: I've been in space the longest time, the longest extended stay in space of any American.

T: Any American in space.

P: That's right.

T: So how tall are you?

P: I'm the longest—well, I'm about five six—but I'm the longest—

T: You can't be the longest.

P: I'm the astronaut who spent the longest time in space.

T: You're the—excuse me, you're the astro*nette*.

P: I'm an astronaut.

T: Astronette.

P: That's a new word.

T: Thank you! I've invented a new word. You can't just have *astronaut*. It makes people think you're a man.

P: It doesn't, actually. There have been many female astronauts and I'm proud to be in their number.

T: Listen, I want you to go to Mars.

P: Are you announcing a Mars mission?

T: Yes, I'm announcing it right now. And I want you to do it as soon as womanly possible. Move the space station to Mars. Step on it.

P: I don't think that's possible.

T: Do you see the dead teacher up there?

P: Excuse me?

T: The one who blew up.

P: No sir.

T: We're on a mission to retrieve her body—

P: From the *Challenger*?

T: And bring it back to Earth so we can bury it with dignity.

P: Sir, if I can be perfectly frank, the whole problem was they didn't make it to space. The *Challenger* crashed into the ocean.

T: That's not what I read.

P: It was one of the saddest days of my life.

T: Well, it's a sad thing, but it was a woman pilot, so you can't— I'm sorry.

P: Sir, this call, I'm told, is to express your congratulations on the work that we're doing on the space station. And if you'd prefer to discuss other subjects, I'm afraid I should return to my work.

T: How do you breathe up there?

P: Air, sir.

T: How?

P: We bring air up and breathe it. And we recycle the carbon dioxide and pump in the oxygen.

T: You gotta send it up? How do you send it up?

P: Well, we have compressed air and chemicals to combine and we have plants here and some of the plants refresh the air. It's a chemistry experiment, sir. It's actually fascinating when you get into the details.

T: Okay, I don't care about it. You have air up there. I don't like the recycling, it's a total myth. This notion of the environmentalists and the tree huggers who are ruining business for everybody. As far as I'm concerned, it could stand to be a little warmer in DC right now. And if the earth gets hotter because of global warming, then we'll all be on beachfront property. Am I right or am I not right?

P: Sir, if I could take this opportunity, I would emphasize to you the reality of global warming and what a complicated issue—

T: If there's one thing I know, it's reality. I was the host of a show called *The Apprentice*!

P: I don't watch much TV.

T: On NBC.

P: As I said, I don't watch a lot of television, but I hear that it was a very well-liked show and I congratulate you on it.

T: Congratulations to me!

P: Yes, sir.

T: You don't get TV up in space, so what do you do?

P: We actually do watch movies.

T: What is—what was the last movie you watched?

P: We watched some old movies. We watched *Casablanca*.

T: Oh, that's a good one. *Casablanca* . . . give me a kiss, Sam, give me a kiss.

P: Yes sir.

T: Here's looking at you, Sam. Play it again, kid. The two great lines from *Casablanca*. And then they found the falcon at the end! I miss the days when we had men like Bogey and Bacall. All of them are gone. Smoking Joe, DiMaggio, Barbara Billingsley, Marilyn Monroe, Old Liz—"Marriage!" Remember when that video came out?

P: No sir.

T: Do you want DirecTV up there? I mean, I gotta imagine the signal's gotta be great. You're right next to the satellites.

P: Actually, no sir, we are actually in a higher orbit than the geostationary satellites that provide DirecTV. Isn't that interesting? So if anything, we could look down at the satellites.

T: Well, that doesn't seem like an interesting movie.

P: Well, it's not a movie. It's our actual perspective here on the edge of space. It's the reality of our scientific mission here to explore—

T: Strange new worlds and seek out new civilizations.

P: Well sir, I actually am a *Star Trek* fan.

T: I love *Star Trek*.

P: You do?

T: Absolutely. Uhura—big piece of ass. Too bad she's black. And Sulu, though, turned out to be a little light in the Asian slippers.

P: Sir, I'm not comfortable with anything you just said. Again, as far as I'm concerned, you're calling the space station to congratulate us on the work we're doing, and we appreciate that sentiment.

T: I have a new plan for space. Have you heard about the Space Force? We're building a Space Force. We have an Air Force, we need a Space Force. Space Force One.

P: I see.

T: A fleet of spaceships that circle the earth, fighting aliens! And ISIS!

P: Well actually, the Russian cosmonauts and the astronauts in NASA both agree that it's inappropriate to militarize outer space. Our countries disagree on many things but we agree on that. Humanity's shared future is in the stars on a peaceful mission of exploration, not the continued warfare that has defined most of our species' existence on Earth.

T: Yeah, tell that to the Klingons. Those people are unforgiving. Babababaaabaabaabaa baaa ba ba ba ba *(hums the* Star Trek *tune)* DoooooOOOo DoooooOOOo DoooooOOOo.

P: I actually remember that episode, sir.

T: It was Spock's pon farr. Every seven years he finally gets horny and needs to get laid. Can you imagine that? You don't have sex for seven years?

P: Well, we're about to round the planet and be out of range because the sun's rising where we are, so we're not going to be able to maintain this channel of communication when we're in direct sunlight.

T: It's night out here!

P: Sir, I'm going to have a hard time explaining this to you in the amount of time we have. But I'm happy to hear that you're a *Trek* fan. I see myself as a bit of a Captain Janeway.

T: Ehh, no. You're more of a Beverly Crusher.

P: Thank you for calling, Mr. President.

T: Hello?!

CALL: LEE NAK-YEON, PRIME MINISTER OF SOUTH KOREA

Trump: Kelsey, make a note for the library: I've been president for a year, and look. The country has no problems.

Kelsey: I'll write that down, but there are still a few problems, though, wouldn't you say?

T: Like what? What's a problem? What's your problem?

K: Infrastructure?

T: We're taking care of the infrastructure. It's going to be big. A big week. I'm saving it for sweeps.

K: Fair enough. What about North Korea? A lot of people are saying that one of the most pressing issues of your presidency will be attempting to negotiate with the North Koreans and trying to broker peace between South and North Korea.

T: It's easy, so easy; Obama was too weak. "Just do the nuclear, who cares." That's what Obama said. I'll show you how easy it is. I'll call the South Korea Guy right now.

T: It's ringing.

Lee Nak-yeon: Hello, the office of Lee Nak-yeon.

T: Who's there?

L: Lee Nak-yeon.

T: Are you having a stroke?

L: This is Lee Nak-yeon's office.

T: Orange you glad I didn't say banana?

L: I'll connect you right with the prime minister.

T: Hello? Hello? Hello? Hello?

L: Hello, yes?

T: Hello?

L: Yes, Mr. President.

T: I was gonna hang up.

L: Oh. Well, I'm glad you didn't. The Olympics went off smashingly, wouldn't you say?

T: I dunno, I don't watch that stuff.

L: Oh. Vice President Pence was here.

T: Yeah, he likes to look at all the ice skating. He's always at the ice skating! Cause he likes the packages on the skaters with the packages, you know what I mean?

L: I'm sorry, my translator is shaking his head.

T: Well, let me tell you about Mike. Mike likes to get in a toboggan and bobsled, you know what I mean? With the whole Jamaican bobsled team. But it's not about going down the mountain. It's just about going down. You get it now?

L: Yes—

T: And the funny thing is, he'd hang gay people from the back of a truck if he could!

L: Yes sir. Well, um—

T: He tells me all the time! He's like, "I'm glad all those people got AIDS in Indiana." I'm like, "Geez, Mike, you're crazy! You shouldn't say stuff like that."

L: Well, Mr. President, I want to offer my sincere thanks. The hard position you took on North Korean aggression since the beginning of your—

T: Oh yeah.

L: —your term has resulted in their softening their stance toward us and had us marching under the same flag at the Olympics. So credit where credit's due. The posturing you used against them seems to have defrosted the relationship between the North and South on our peninsula.

T: Oh, whoa, I got burger meat defrosting upstairs. I'm making my own Big Macs tonight! No progress on the wife, though.

L: Yes sir. Well, I'm not sure if the language barrier is getting in the way, but I'm trying to give you a compliment on your posture.

T: You know something? The posture I took with North Korea was to lean a little further than I normally do. And I put my arms back! That's a different posture than I've ever held.

L: Yes sir.

T: Hey, how was that Kim Jong-un? Un. The first, in French. What's his sister like?

L: Well, I certainly didn't meet her, sir.

T: Oh, wow, really? That was the whole point. I thought she'd come to South Korea and you guys would fall in love! You'd get together and then you'd make a baby. And it's the first baby that's South Korean and North Korean, and then that boy would be the golden boy! And then Eddie Murphy shows up, and he's like, "Whoa, whatchu talkin bout, I'm Eddie Murphy! I don't do no golden child!" But he does. And then he learns to believe after he meets an Asian girl. And then the world's problems are solved. The golden child frees everybody!

L: I had to switch translators in the middle of that, sir. One of them gave up.

T: *Beverly Hills Cop III* is pretty good too. Lots of people say it's the worst of the series but I think the whole idea of being stuck at an amusement park was a way more interesting idea than *II*, which I think let a lot of things down. I mean, let's face it. That chase at the end was pretty boring. What happened to Eddie Murphy?

L: Yes sir. I got the box of DVDs that you mailed to me.

T: Yeah, did you get *Norbit*?

L: I believe so, sir.

T: You see the one with Robert De Niro?

L: I haven't watched any of them at all, sir.

T: Well, you should watch them. Don't you Koreans love movies? It's all you do, make movies.

L: I personally have my hands full with the business of state.

T: Oooooh . . . Gangnam style! Oomp oomp run dun dun dun dun. Ooh, Gangnam style!

L: You know, Gangnam is a neighborhood in Seoul.

T: Superbad! Cause I got soooooul, I'm superbad. (pause) Hello?

L: The Chinese president is on the other line. I'm actually very tempted to take this call, my translators are nodding.

T: No, hold on. Let's talk. You don't want to tell me what music you like? That's fine. So what happens now with Jong-un?

L: We'll plan a summit, then cancel the summit, then have a quick summit where nothing happens and then wind up where we were.

T: And then we can finally have peace in the Middle East.

NORTH KOREA SUMMIT ITINERARY (6/12/2018)

0800: POTUS wakes up, check like count on Trudeau slam tweet

0830: Flip coin to decide whether to have summit or not

(IF TAILS)

0900: POTUS to Air Force One

1000: Tweet picture of crushed Canada Dry can from official White House account (tag Trudeau)

1100: Announce summit canceled, fly to Washington DC

(IF HEADS)

0845: Remind POTUS we are in Singapore, listen to POTUS Singapore song

0900: POTUS Breakfast: Eggs Benedict, take photo of Canadian Bacon on floor (tag Trudeau)

0915: POTUS Flashcards: DPRK, KIM JONG UN, PENNINSULA, HANDSHAKE, BOMB

1000: POTUS private screening of CHOICE VIDEO produced to show KJU (Summary: 2 possible futures for DPRK peace or war). Have Aerosmith "Cryin'" music video on standby if POTUS scared or bored.

1020: POTUS meets with BOLTON in NO MUSTACHE DISGUISE

1030: Arrive Venue, listen to POTUS Sentosa song

1045: POTUS samples beverage alternatives for customary toast: NB
ALL PRUNE JUICE per physician

1100: POTUS counts steps in meeting room, does "Here's Donny"
through double doors

1115: Free Wander (per Kelly: DO NOT LET POTUS WATCH TV, WILL
TRY TO PICK UP ACCENT)

1130: Back pat coaching in anteroom

1200: SUMMIT BEGINS

  -Open with a joke

  -Remarks

  -Joint Statement

  -Handshake

1400: SUMMIT ENDS

1415: Lure KJU into limousine photo booth (props, voice bubbles on
table nearby)

1500: POTUS private inspection KJU Toilet Car

1520: Second handshake

1600: Board Air Force One

1700: Wheels up

1800: NORAD provides coordinates for stateside flock of Canada
Geese, Air Force One intercepts for engine intake. Tweet photo, tag
Trudeau.

CALL: EMMANUEL MACRON, PRESIDENT OF FRANCE

Trump: Who's this?

Emmanuel Macron: Emmanuel Macron, Mr. President. The president of France.

T: Did you call me?

E: Yes sir.

T: Oh.

E: We had a call scheduled, sir.

T: I made a phone call, I was picking up the call. I was calling this woman.

E: Very well, sir.

T: I was picking the phone up to make a call, and then you were on the line!

E: I'm sure that was not the case, sir, I'm sure that your staff sat you down with the telephone for this call.

T: I don't know about that, I'm not even sure it's for me.

E: France is one of your country's oldest and dearest friends. And I'm calling to implore you to remain a party to the Paris Accord.

T: Of course you want me to come to your party, it's in Paris. You don't have to go anywhere.

E: It's an agreement about Climate Change, saving the world from the devastating effects of climate change.

T: Climate change? I like it just the way it is. Don't touch that thermostat!

E: Sir, there are more than one hundred fifty countries in the accord. And the heads of state are unanimous about the risks we face.

T: Heads of state. They're all—we're all heads of state. And we head the state up very well. All fifty states. First off, though, I'm the biggest head of state. I'm the big guy. And in that way, I'm all your boss!

E: Not exactly, sir. First among equals, perhaps, as far as the Western alliance is concerned.

T: Last time I checked, you guys were really hurting in World War II.

E: Last time you checked World War II, it was equally distant in the past, too.

T: What? I don't want to do math.

E: There's not much to check on regarding the Second World War.

T: What about Vietnam? You guys lost that one too. Bunch of losers.

E: All right, sir. I don't believe this is a productive topic of conversation.

T: I'm kidding. Listen. You need to lighten up. You French people, you're all so serious. You're all about the love and the baguettes and the wine and the cheese.

E: I see you've spent some time here, sir.

T: I was just at NATO, which is a province in France.

E: No sir. You were in Paris, sir.

T: Bless you.

E: Well, I believe we could have had a more productive NATO meeting, the meeting of the allied states, sir.

T: We had a wonderful meeting, it was one of the great meetings. Going there to see all the history, and there's so much—I mean, think about that. There are Neanderthals that lived in caves, so deep under the ground. And they were having sex with human ladies!

E: That's true, sir. Some interesting science has come out about that in the past few years. That modern humans are descended from hominids who mated with Denisovan man.

T: I don't know—dinosaur man? I hope not. I don't know about that. What's that?

E: It's interesting that there were multiple species of humans on the planet before modern man emerged.

T: Black, Asian, Jewish . . .

E: It doesn't quite correspond exactly that way.

T: I don't know. There might have been a lot of different humans, but just on like *The Apprentice*, only one group of humans could win. And it turned out to be us humans! But I'll tell you this: Those Neanderthals. I mean, they must have had great personalities, because they were very ugly. So for them to get some human-lady pussy? Unbelievable.

E: I see, sir. Perhaps it was ugly humans who were sleeping with Neanderthal women.

T: Excuse me, I don't think there were any ugly humans. Neanderthals are ugly. You ever see a Neanderthal lady? I saw one at the Natural History Museum. She had tits down to her knees!

E: Well, that's what I'm saying, sir. Perhaps it was human men who were pursuing the Neanderthal women.

T: I doubt it. Are you kidding me? What's wrong with you?

E: Well, I don't know, then. Perhaps, yes, it was charming Neanderthal men who were able to seduce human women.

T: That's exactly right. Listen, I have a question. Would you swap out your hottie wife for some tit-draggin' Neanderthal biddie?

E: No sir, of course I wouldn't.

T: Well, there you go, case in point. But some guy with a big brow and a billion dollars in a Swiss bank account, trust me. She'd be legs-up tits-down in two seconds.

E: All right, sir. I think we should talk about our mutual security.

T: Don't you French people like talking about shit like this?

E: Not in so many words, sir.

T: So don't you guys like to swap wives?

E: Some people enjoy that practice, Mr. President, but I am not among them.

T: I don't know. Macaroon? You're a dodgy one. And your wife is an old lady so your priorities are all over the place. But let's put it this way. We saw all the great people in Germany and Europe. We saw Merkel, you, the British lady, all the people from all the countries in Europe together in one place.

E: Well, yes sir, but I should point out that you declined to put the support of your people and your country and your military behind NATO, the most successful military alliance in human history.

T: I gave that speech where I talked about how great all the allies were during World War II, and then immediately the next day I said how useless NATO was and how we should pull out! That makes perfect sense.

E: I'm afraid it doesn't, sir, and I would have to request that you make a stronger statement in support of the alliance. I will remind you that the one time NATO's Article 5 was invoked was after the United States was attacked and the allies joined you in battle in Afghanistan.

T: They didn't join me, I didn't fight over there. I got bone spurs!

E: Your people.

T: They're not my people.

E: Your military.

T: It's not my military then.

E: The US army.

T: Uh-huh, what about them?

E: We fight side by side, shoulder to shoulder as brothers in arms.

T: *(singing)* From the halls of Montezuma, to the revenge of Tripoli.

E: Yes, sir.

T: Remember that? Where's Tripoli, in France?

E: It's in Libya.

T: What?!

E: It's in Libya.

T: Where is it now?

E: Tripoli is in Libya. But my staff tells me you're considering making a visit to the South of France. Have we had the pleasure of your company before, sir?

T: I don't know. I've been to Europe but I never pay attention to the borders.

E: I see.

T: But I'll say this. If we're going to the South of France, it's gonna be a beautiful villa. We're staying in a beautiful villa, it's so wonderful there, with the people. You might be weak-kneed little cowards, but you know how to screw and how to chew, and that's one thing we can all agree on.

E: Well, thank you, sir.

T: You have dandruff on your right shoulder.

E: How can you know this?

T: A lady never tells.

INTERVIEW: DAVOS CONFERENCE

Trump: I love the Davos. It's an incredible place. All the bigwigs come here and they think they're the biggest deal in town just because they have that old Europe money. They act all snooty and "can I have a crumpet with my little egg pot?" give me a break.

Kelsey: So why come here?

T: I read the cover of an incredible book about how these Davos Euro People are Lizards! Many people are saying they are lizards dressed like humans. They come to Europe where there is no air conditioning so it's hot and moist so they can lay their eggs. And because of that there are so many rituals. But it's mainly for the Davos Conference. The Davos sex conference.

K: Why do you say sex conference?

T: Haven't you been to the parties?

K: No sir, I've never been.

T: Oh my god. Let me tell you something. You think these people are freaky? First off, we show up and then they take me into a room and they go, you gotta put your hand on this five-star thing. It looked like a bunch of triangles tied together. And they go, you gotta prick your finger! And I go, I already did a blood test when I became president. And I've got it all. All the good blood. I'll tell you, all the great blood. And the many blood diseases. I've got hemoglobins, hobgoblins, everything. Then they make me put my hand on this little Star of Jared but it was missing one of the corners.

K: A Pentagram.

T: Uh huh. So I put my hand on it, and then they made me say an oath, and I always love saying oaths. I'll say any oath you want. I did the Pledge of Allegiance. They said, "No, repeat this other stuff." I had to say, "*Santo sangui*" something. Who knows. Then they put you in a robe—which I love, I thought I was getting a spa treatment. Then they open this door, and oh boy, everyone was just going at it! You shoulda seen it.

The sprinkler system came on out on the balcony. I got soaked! I said, "Oh boy oh boy, all this water's on me!" So I went back inside, the party took a real turn! Everyone's in masks and hoods. There's a guy with a synthesizer, he's just hitting the same note over and over again! I said, "Play something new!" I went up and requested "Only the Good Die Young" by Billy Joel. He didn't know it! I mean, who doesn't know that song!? Also, everyone was looking at me cause they were standing in a circle. I walked right through it! Anyway, there was this hot naked lady. She looked like a *Sports Illustrated* swimsuit model. She was sitting in the middle of the room. There were two guys in red cloaks, one guy in a purple cloak, and they all had these weird penis masks on. Now, you know I don't go for that weird stuff, okay? I'm vanilla. My favorite thing is to bring a girl into my room, make love to her, and then show her the *Donahue* tape, the VHS, and then catch a few Z's. Listen, the reason they call it missionary position is because you're on a mission: to finish, and lie down. So then they start yelling and it sounds like they're talking backward on a record! It's like this, it was like, [GIBBERISH]. They were talking backward. So then I tried to play it forward. But it didn't work and I got bored because I had no bars so I pulled the guy's mask up, and he kept saying, "No No No!" He was the Prime Minister of Norway! So I say, "How you doing, your wife's so beautiful, where is she, I gotta see her." He says, "Please don't ever say you saw me here." And I told him that I would never say a thing. Except in this interview. But that's one time.

So then I got bored with the circle. There was too much smoke. A guy was walking around with a big incense chain, swinging it around. So I wandered farther into the room. Would you believe it? I go in other rooms, and painted on the floor, in what looked like red paint, was one of those giant Jewish stars that's missing a point!

K: Another pentagram, we covered this.

T: Well, in this room, there were four or five naked women, all at the different points, each one wearing a different mask symbolizing the seasons of the year, with a fifth season representing the all-encompassing season of time. That's what it said on the pamphlet. No one would talk to me, so I just went around saying, "Good to meet you, Donald Trump." I kicked over a bunch of candles and they said, "You're breaking the salt line." I said, "What are you talking about?" Apparently when you do magic, the salt protects the circle inside. I kicked that salt all over the place because it was a total mess! And they said I brought about a thousand years of death and blood on the fire. But I said, "Whatever!" I don't believe in that stuff. I heard another piano, and I went into another room. Maybe this guy will play "Philadelphia Freedom" by Elton John! So I walked by piles of writhing people all having the dirtiest sex you've ever seen. I mean, this was dirty. All I'm gonna say is there was definitely butt juice mixing with regular juice. Grinding, moaning, praying to gods whose names I can't even pronounce. I couldn't pronounce them, but I'll say this: It stunk in there. And if I were a god, I wouldn't go anywhere near this orgy. Then I got up to the pianist, and I said, "'Philadelphia Freedom,' huh, buddy?" And he played it! Boy this orgy took a turn.

He was slamming out "Philadelphia Freedom" and these people got up and they started moving! And the real Elton John pulled his mask up, and he was there too! I promised him I wouldn't tell anybody I saw him there too. So the real Elton John and the Billy Joel did one of their famous Madison Square Garden duets at Davos. They pushed their pianos together right there in the Illuminati party. I said, "These Illuminati are great! This is where all the deals get made!" We had a great time. It was a two-hour concert. At the end, for an encore, they played "New York State of Mind." Finally, someone with a giant eagle mask came up and said, "Mr. President, could you please come with me?" They led me out, but not before I pulled as many masks up on as many people as I could see. And here's the top five: Nathaniel Rothschild, World Bank president Kristalina Georgieva, Dick Cheney, Martin Mull, and Hillary Clinton. And boy, did we laugh. The end! The end!

K: Why are you saying "the end"?

T: Cause that's the end of the story!

CALL: TIM COOK, CEO OF APPLE

Trump: And in the Garden of Eden . . . there was an apple. Hello, it's me!

Tim Cook: Good morning, Mr. President.

T: Good morning, Mr. Jobs.

C: Tim Cook.

T: Oh, whoops! Steve Jobs. Too many Cooks in the kitchen, make the jobs dead. We used to have so many Jobs, and now you're a Cook. And that's what happened to America, and it's a huge problem. Now, you're different from the other guy who ran Apple, right?

C: That's right, we miss Steve tremendously and he meant so much to the company. But he passed away and now it's my job to carry on his legacy. Now, the reason for this call, I'm told, is that you want my thoughts on a new jobs program.

T: Yeah, but you're not him.

C: Oh, I—

T: When are you going to die?

C: I hope not any time soon, sir! (laughs)

T: How do you know?

C: Well, I guess I don't know. Do you know?

T: Yeah.

C: You know when you're going to.

T: Of course I do.

C: When, sir?

T: In the future.

C: Well, I suppose that's true of me too. (laughs)

T: What are you laughing at?

C: Oh, it's polite laughter to cover parts of the conversation that would otherwise be silent.

T: My uncle went to Nikola Tesla's room after he died and took all his papers, so I know science.

C: I've heard that story, sir. That's a fascinating story.

T: And that's how I know when I'm going to die!

C: What a strange coincidence.

T: I know I'm gonna die because my uncle used a time viewer to see the future.

C: I see, sir, well we'll have to invent one of those. (laughs) Maybe that's a little bit of technology we can put in the next model of the iPhone. (laughs)

T: Why would you do that? I don't understand.

C: Well, if you could try to look through time I guess that would be a good feature for a smartphone, sir.

T: No, not really. The screen's too small.

C: How big was the screen that your uncle saw?

T: It was like a small portable tube television.

C: Well, that's about the same resolution as our Super Retina displays on the iPhone X.

T: Ooh, that's sexy.

C: We're just making them a little bigger, then a little smaller again, then we're gonna make the pixels dense, then we're gonna spread them out, and then we're gonna pack them in again. And then we're introducing more great new tech, like you can make yourself into a cartoon pumpkin now.

T: Wow. Really? I've always wanted to be a cartoon pumpkin.

C: Or, instead of just sending a boring voice mail with just audio, you can send a cartoon of yourself as a piece of shit murmuring to itself.

T: Wow! I love that! That's so much more fun. That makes voice mails fun to do again!

C: That's right. We're adding cameras and taking cameras away. We're gonna make it sharp-edged and then we're gonna round the edges again, and then we're gonna make them a little thinner, then a little thicker, then we're going to give it a little twist, and then—

T: Oh boy, you're talking about my morning in the toilet. Listen. Apple has done so much. They've made so many great products, and let's say it, quite frankly, a lot of them when you weren't there. It's true that you got a lot to live up to. I mean, you've got a genius. You've got a guy you gotta live up to, and I understand that. Because when you become the president, you live up to a lot of history, and there's a lot of history, and a lot of the greats came before you. But you've gotta become the best. And some say, a lot of people are saying, that I'm the best president that's ever lived. And someday they're going to say that about you! And eventually you'll get to change your name to Jobs! And then you'll be the new Steve Jobs!

C: Well, I guess that's one possibility, sir. (laughs)

T: What's happening over there?! Are you at a party?

C: No sir. Just, I love chatting.

T: Okay . . . Now, the iPhone X is for pornography.

C: Well, we do have a private browsing mode if that's what you're looking for today, sir. But it's for everyone. It's for everyone to do whatever they want. It's for exploring the limits of their own creativity—

T: How?

C: Apps?

T: You don't know?

C: We used to do GarageBand and Final Cut Pro, but I don't know.

T: I don't understand it. Now I have a phone, and the reason I was calling today is that I can't find my drafts on Twitter.

C: Oh, you're calling for tech support?

T: What? I guess so. Yeah, can you help me get my drafts on Twitter?

C: Well actually, Twitter's a third-party app; we don't directly support all the apps that run on the phone—

T: You gotta be kidding me. You don't know how Twitter works?

C: I do know how Twitter works, you know I don't really tweet personally—

T: You don't?

C: And they're a separate company from us, so—

T: Okay, so? Tell me how to do it.

C: I think there's probably a folder, you could go up to the root folder structure and find the folder that says "drafts."

T: What the hell are you talking about? Tell me how to push buttons.

C: You could probably go up a level and find a drafts folder.

T: Up a level? What?

C: Up a level in the folder structure.

T: I don't understand.

C: Or you could just go—

T: Where are my photos?!

C: You could go onto a search engine and say, "Access Twitter drafts" and someone's probably written a how-to article about it, I'd imagine.

T: I don't have the time. Where are my photos?

C: It depends on the settings on your phone. Your photos are in the phone, or if you use iCloud photo sharing, we store the full resolution—

T: I don't do the cloud. I don't do the cloud.

C: Well you should, sir. It can save you space on your phone—

T: I don't like the cloud.

C: You can save a little space on your phone and then if we ever decide to change the way we store the photos, we'll just delete them forever.

T: So where are my photos now?

T: Well, if they were on MobileMe photo sharing, they're gone. If they're on iCloud photo sharing, they're up there now, at least until we decide to do Photos a different way. And if they're on your phone then they're just on your phone.

T: I look at the phone and I see a picture.

C: Good, well that's at least one photo you have on there.

T: I think that's me on the phone. I think I'm taking a picture of myself.

C: Sir, in addition to your jobs program—

T: Rest in peace.

C: I actually wanted to talk to you about the tariffs on aluminum and some of the other metals.

T: Absolutely. The tariffs, they're killing us.

C: Well, the tariffs are going to really severely impact our business, but I should just warn you, businessman to businessman—

T: I'm a businessman!

C: The people most affected by the retaliatory tariffs from China against our country now that we've started this trade war are likely going to be some of your constituents, sir. Some of the people who voted for you.

T: No, those people are coal miners. They don't know about aluminum. Do you know they call it "Ah-loo-minee-um" in Britain?

C: I did know that, sir. But the retaliatory tariffs from China are going to severely affect agriculture in some of the states that voted for you—

T: What metal is "retaliatory"?

C: Retaliatory isn't a metal, sir. It's a description of the way the Chinese are going to behave.

T: Is that Chinese?

C: Yes, sir.

T: For what?

C: Well, the word isn't Chinese, sir. It's a description in English of how the Chinese are going to react. They're going to retaliate.

T: Well why didn't you say "react"?

C: I did.

T: Why say the other one?

C: It more correctly and precisely describes what I'm trying to say.

T: Not to me. It's totally confusing.

C: That's true. I guess that it could be my fault.

T: Boy, I wish Steve Jobs was alive. He wouldn't be having a conversation like this.

C: I think he would.

T: No he wouldn't.

C: I think he might.

T: He was a straight shooter.

C: I'm a straight shooter, sir.

T: You're a straight suitor? Oh. Are you here to court my daughter?

C: No sir, I'm gay, as it happens.

T: Oh I know it happens. Believe me. Here's the point. China's hitting us with the aluminum, they're hitting us with the steel, and we're gonna hit back. And you need to make the phones. And the phones need to be made of the aluminum and the retaliatory, and all the metals that go into it. And they make the apps. And the apps run, and they're fast, and we like to type in them. And you like to type in the technology. You wanna keep making the cyber and keep making the phone go bigger and smaller, then you're gonna have to make a deal. And you're gonna have to go along with this China thing. You're just gonna have to ride it out.

C: I understand, sir. Don't say I didn't warn you.

T: One more thing.

C: Yes?

T: Is Siri hot?

C: Between you and me? Yes. She's a 10.

T: Whoa, wow! Really?!

CALL: ANGELA MERKEL, CHANCELLOR OF GERMANY

Trump: What's this ring? This isn't the right ring. Hello? Hello?

Angela Merkel: Hello, this is Angela Merkel.

T: What?

A: Angela Merkel.

T: What's that, a disease?

A: No, I'm the chancellor of Germany.

T: Oh, heil Hitler.

A: Oh, of course.

T: Don't you have to say that when you talk to Germans?

A: No, not in a long time. Those are days we wish to put behind us, Mr. President. The German people send their regards to the American people—

T: Oh yeah, the American people say hi back. So did you follow Hitler? Was it Hitler, then you?

A: No, Mr. President.

T: What was it like working for him? Did you work out of the bunker?

A: Mr. President, please.

T: I got a bunker!

A: I'm calling because your representatives from your administration have recently been attempting to negotiate a unilateral trade deal with Germany and I wish to remind you again that the only deals we can make, the only trade deals we can make, are with the European Union. We are exclusive to the European common market—

T: Well forget that.

A:—and you'll have to make a trade deal with the European Union—

T: Who's talking about that?

A:—not the individual countries of the union, sir.

T: Excuse me, excuse me, first off, who in my administration, you tell me right now, who has talked to you about any unilateral deal?

A: It was one of your delegations to the G5, a lower level discussion.

T: Give me a name.

A: I'll have to make some inquiries.

T: I'll fire whoever it is. Opening his mouth. I'm the only one who does unilateral.

A: Well, we can't do unilateral, that's my point.

T: I do unilateral. You don't do unilateral.

A: Well you can't. You can't unilaterally make a deal with Germany, you have to bilaterally make a deal with the European Union.

T: Of course, Europeans, it's all about the bi everything. Let me tell you something. I get that you Europeans do weird negotiations that are bilateral, but here in the United States it's between one man and one woman. And I'm the man, and you're the woman, and we're going to make our deal.

A: I can't make a deal outside of the European Union.

T: We need to dissolve the European Union—

A: No we do not.

T:—immediately.

A: No we do not.

T: You guys did the Brexit.

A: No we didn't.

T: When are you gonna get out of there.

A: We didn't do the Brexit. In fact, we're hoping that the people of the United Kingdom will change their minds especially now that we know there was Russian money behind the Brexit campaign.

T: The Brexit people are a great people who live in Germany who want freedom for themselves. I've seen them and the documentaries about them. They speak loudly in beer halls. They make great speeches about bringing Germany back to the people and back to the pure blood that made them great, and if the Russians want to help them there, or here, I'll be the first to say give me that money, and get them in to the G7.

A: I think you're conflating a few things, Mr. President.

T: The Germans are a great people. Great symbols! And rallies. We'd love to have rallies like you guys have. And I love the uniforms you have, really slick. You guys have a lot going for you. Why you gonna give it up? You got it all. You got the fashion, you got the symbols, you got the great leadership. I mean, you work for the guy! And now it's time for you to carry on his legacy.

A: I can assure you I am not making any attempt to carry on Adolf Hitler's legacy.

T: No, you should make it your own. I always believed that. It's very hard, especially when you take over for a male CEO, as charismatic as he was, and let's face it, on this phone call, it's clear you're as boring as a wood plank. But the truth is, you gotta distance yourself, separate yourself, but at the same time, don't drop what the guy had. He had a great economy, great speeches. People say Hitler was bad, but the guy was a vegetarian! He was a vegetarian! A goddamn hippie! A Hippy Hippy Hitler! He also unified an entire people behind a nationalist ethnocentric cause! I'm not a vegetarian, and I did that. Hello?

A: Yes, sir.

T: Lemme tell you, let's make a deal now. You do whatever you need to do, tell the union. I want steel tariffs to go up thirty percent. I want to deal with you on electronics, on the cyber. I want to make sure the computers are all aligned. Everyone has the right computer. I wanna make sure Germans can come here, they can bring their bread and pretzels and schnitzels, and in return, we will export all the hot dogs, and all the good stuff that you guys like.

A: Again, I'm not in a position to make that deal. You'll have to talk to the European council.

T: Why are you crawling up my ass like this? Can I ask you that? Why is it that every woman I talk to, there's a big problem. Why are you making it such a big problem? Okay, Angelo?

A: Angela.

T: If you say so. Now, listen. Europe and Germany have had a great relationship, and so has America, with the United States. We all have the same interests at heart. And we need to be kinder to Russia. We need to be nicer to Russia, we must involve Russia in everything, the EU, the E-Z Pass, the EA Sports. The more we get Russia involved, the better off we'll be. NATO is bye-bye! Angela, who's the boss?! I am! And I say we make a deal. I wanna get little shoes from you people. You have the best shoes. I wanna go— You have a Black Forest cake?

A: Yes sir, I was going to have one for lunch.

T: Jesus. Lemme tell you, that's your first problem.

A: With my staff.

T: Okay, let's face it, Angela. I'll say your name right. You said you're going to have the whole cake for lunch, then after the fact you said you're going to share it with your staff.

A: Fine, we'll make a deal.

T: There we go.

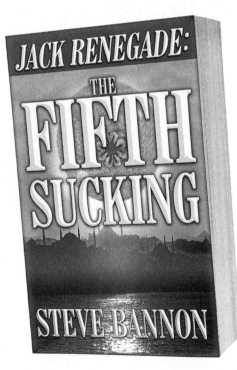

Excerpts from "The Fifth Sucking" Trilogy

BOOK ONE

The true story of Western civilization can be found in the halls of the libraries of Amenti and in the secret book of Thoth. In the legendary book of Hermitca, our European Western heritage is informed by thousands of years of prehistoric dominance brought forth by the high priestesses of Atlantis and carried by the great Western traditions of Plato, Socrates, and Aristotle. In all these mysteries there is one common cycle. There are many turnings, each one happening every 32,000 years according to the great star calendar of the ancients. Each turning is an alchemical process by which mankind is transformed and refined into a higher state being. Only those of select breed and genetic purity have the advantageous ability to recognize these turnings. I have often written of the fourth turning in human civilization, but it has been revealed to me that there was another turning. It turns out the fourth turning turned earlier, it turned completely over, like a pancake or a waffle. This pancake turning occurs symbolically in the destruction of the great pillars Joachim and Boaz, known in the vernacular as the Twin Towers, on September 11th, 2001. It was this ceremony of ritual sacrifice, prefigured in the bombing of the garage below an harmonic eight years before, that charred those pure souls into the husks of humanity that would save Western civilization for the twenty-first century and beyond, for this is called the Fifth Sucking. By some in the modern era it is known as a rapture, but this is too foolish and simple a term for the grand design of the true architect of our universe.

Could I simply tell you what the Fifth Sucking is? Indeed, I could. But man is a storyteller. And stories have characters. Persona means mask and masks are fiction, so in the great tradition of Homer, this epic is better sung.

Jack Renegade whipped his 2018 Lamborghini Huracán down the winding roads of the Amalfi Coast. It was a typical drive for him: High speed, hot thrills, and all the excitement that came with being the former political adviser to the president of the United States. He had been out of the business for more than a year. It had sucked him dry. It was yet another series in a string of disappointments resulting from his being unappreciated and misunderstood by those he had supported with his loyalty and labor. He knew that the man at the top, the big boss, the guy that mattered—he could reach him and hear him. But it was all the flotsam and jetsam of the fallen world surrounding him that troubled Jack Renegade so deeply.

So lost in thought, Jack realized too late that he was heading straight for a cliff. He threw the wheel. His Huracán went into auto-steering lock mode. It was specially designed for moments like this. Jack knew he could get lost in thought. Those thoughts made him money, and money made power. So the truth is, sometimes he had to turn over control. The car slid over the gravel, the back edge of the Huracán just barely dusting the guardrail, shooting sparks into the summer air.

Jack muttered to himself, "Regulations." He knew the Amalfi coast as one of the great sanctuaries of the Knights Templar and their twelfth-century crusade toward Jerusalem. These great knights, men who slept with each other and spent their time in piety and filth knowing that bringing glory to God was worth their great sacrifice. The Templar talisman that dangled from the rearview mirror reminded Jack that he was a part of this important lineage of martyrdom and bloody conquest. The car rolled to a stop, just at the edge of the cliff.

"Another close one," Jack thought as he stepped out of the car.

"Perfect timing," said a familiar voice from behind a rock. It was Gerhardt Bertolf, an art collector and practitioner of dark magic and the ancient rituals of the days of old. He appeared as a wizard, like Merlin from the heath, and Jack knew he had something up his sleeve. This meeting had been set for months. It was time for Jack to get back in the fold. But the only way he could would be to discover the lost tome of the Fifth Sucking, its text long forgotten by its rightful heirs. His journey had just begun, but he was already weary and ready to weep. And he knew that between him and Bertolf, only one of them would survive the night . . .

BOOK TWO

Jack didn't think he'd find himself in this part of Boston again. Last time he was in Southie he left the next morning with scrapes on both knuckles and a real shiner, but he was better for it. If he could scrap with those Southie boys, he could take anything. But here he was, once again, walking by the Purple Shamrock, one of the most notable bars in all of South Boston. And there was a little secret that none of the locals knew. This place had been the original lodge of the master Freemasons of the York Rite.

The lodge closed in 1781, soon after George Washington became president. He had been the master of the lodge and there was no reason for them to stay aboveground, as certain secrets were best kept buried. This had been a local haunt for Jack Renegade, back in his Harvard days. All the other stuffed suits went to the Tasty or spent their nights listening to jazz and seeing plays at the ART. But Jack Renegade had no time to waste on trifles. He didn't take a cab from Cambridge to Southie, but a series of bus connections like a commoner. He rode with the people to hone his understanding of why certain tribes weren't meant to be together. They understood that in Southie, it was in their blood. Hell, they were stoning buses up until 1976. It's always been lost in translation, but these folks knew that it would be better for people to stay with their own. By staying with your tribe you gain power, and by gaining power you have position. The liberal elites of this world have spent thirty years diluting that power, creating the illusion of liberation by integration, when in fact Renegade knew that the secret recipe for total power and absoluteness was to separate the groups thereby allowing them to flourish.

"Let's face it, white Europeans have brought more to this country than any-one else," Jack had groaned many a time in this bar sitting on his favorite stool next to the MegaTouch. "But the most important thing we brought, beyond everything else, was civility and order. A fragile sense of decorum that can be shattered all too easily by the tribal, subhuman behavior of the refugees and former slaves that populated the city." When the barback had heard enough, Renegade would sing "Auld Lang Syne" and settle his tab.

This time, as Jack stood by the side entrance, wisps of dry snowflakes knocking on his craterous nose, he knew he had to go in and confront a part of his past, and maybe heal the wound of loves long gone.

The fiddle whined like a buzzsaw against fresh Vermont wood. A man's foot tapped on the small stage. This Irish fiddle brigade was marching into musical battle and woe be to any who would try to stop them. Their onslaught was a series of simple Celtic tunes, classic sounds that communicated a darker lost secret. "They should be called Celtic runes," Jack said to the college-aged boy playing Golden Tee. "Because each song is a combination in code to unlock a mystery." The ancient Irish people are the most misunderstood. Everyone forgets that they were connected with the shadow realms and se-cret worlds that surround us and intersect invisibly to impact our everyday lives. The Irish knew the secret whistles that blow through the collective soul of mankind, and they possess the chain of keys to reshaping the universe around us, esoteric knowledge lost to the annals of modernity. The last ves-tiges are these simple Irish tunes, pounded out in the moist, smoke-filled air of the Purple Shamrock on a pre-Christmas evening in South Boston. It was somehow fitting that Jack moved his body along to them on the night he was about to meet his destiny . . .

BOOK THREE

Montana. Known for its retreats for the wealthy elites, the media types who have to get away from it all after they get in your head. Jack found this a strange place to find himself searching for the keys to the Fifth Sucking. But he was at home among the hard-working cattle-driving strong virile men.

Lana Lopez removed her blouse in the Penthouse of the Red Roof Inn. She didn't mind that Jack was watching. Although there was no passion between them anymore, it had once burned hot. And still she felt those embers tickling her insides when they were alone in a hotel room. Jack needed her support now more than ever, and she knew what she had to do. As he admired her supple form, he almost forgot that they were mere hours away from entering a secret, long-lost cave that was guarded by the white giants of an ancient age. The mission would put them both in danger. But Jack's courage sprung from love of country. He did everything out of loyalty to the white Europeans who had been so subjugated by the powerful media elites and the multiculturalism that ruled the day. If only Jack could show the world the Sucking, then they would understand the need for the return to a simple way of life. His satellite phone rang, breaking the charged silence.

President Trum sat at his desk in the Oval Office clutching the handset of a telephone on a secret line that would connect him directly to Jack. He dismissed his vice president, a weak-willed, simpleminded man of queer nature. His false piety was only matched by his inability to project masculinity. It was a shame that Trum had to be surrounded by such weak men, but there was one person who could act as a counterbalance. Jack Renegade was convinced that the president would have been his brother if he could have been. A Renegade not just in name but in soul. But these days the big man was in a bind. He had to serve the powers that brought him to power. So Jack's role was that of the North Star; he oriented the president back to ancient, immutable ideals. To the rest of the world, Jack was off the grid. Renegade was nowhere to be found. But it was for moments like these that Trum had the phone line installed.

"How's it going down there, Renegade? We sure miss you up here. I got a bag of pork rinds with your name on it."

"Ha ha, Mr. President. Great to hear from you again. I want you to know the investigation is going well, but we're going to need three of your top-tier CIA operatives to join us for this excursion."

Trum laughed to himself for a moment. He picked up another pork rind and popped it into his mouth. "I've got one better for you. A private security service that isn't corrupted. We can't trust the Deep State. So we've gone even deeper. What have you found out so far?"

"The caves are a series of chambers that lead deeper than any sonar can detect. I think I found it."

"You mean—"

"Yes. The Gateway. The Gateway to the subterranean halls of Amenti that have the secret emerald scrolls that should provide us with the last pieces of information we need to present the revelation world."

"Tell me the truth. You're enjoying your vacation with Lana."

"I can't help it, sir. I do enjoy a good woman once in a while."

Trum scribbled "10" down on a piece of paper. "I can tell you exactly what she's like. And I want my turn if you get a chance."

"Sure. You know Lana understands the deal." Jack couldn't help himself. It was a fantasy he didn't like to entertain. But the idea of sharing Lana with such a powerful leader as Trum gave him rustling in the underbrush. He stood sweating at the edge of the balcony, knowing that inside she was willing to offer herself to him, or to both of them. He'd circumspectly brought it up to her once before and her words echoed in his mind: "If that's what it's going to take to get you going, I guess I'd think about it." Even now he knew Lana could practically read his mind from the interior room, but he could never share the depths of his desires aloud, or at all.

Trum's voice broke through Jack's ruminations. "I wish you the best of luck. Godspeed. And remember, you're an American hero no matter what you come back with." This was all business. This was the business of saving the world. This was about the Fifth Sucking, not the first fucking.

"Sir, I won't let you down."

"I know you won't. At ease."

Just then the blast of helicopter blades filled the air. Jack knew it was time to go. He beckoned to Lana, who came out, still in her slip. A rope lowered, and they grabbed ahold. There was no landing pad inconspicuous enough for them to be picked up, so instead it had to be a quick escape. They would fly past Bozeman over the Hyalite foothills to the cave site.

As they held each other aloft in the air, Lana and Jack looked at each other. Sure, was Jack in the best shape of his life? No. But she saw past that. She saw past the psoriasis cracks of his face, and the bulbous blisters of welled-up bacteria and pus hanging off his body that Jack called "work scars." His belly touched her. She had never felt hotter. It was good to have a real man next to her, not some lithe, hairless, muscle-bound creep, but a real man. A man who knew to wear a coat on top of a shirt on top of a shirt on top of a turtleneck. A man who knew no limit to the variety of khakis he could wear. She reached out to kiss his lips but Jack placed his single wartless finger between their mouths.

"There's no time for this. We have the business of mankind to attend to. And once mankind is attended to, your needs come second."

CALL: THERESA MAY

Trump: Who am I talking to now?

May: Mr. President, this is Theresa May.

T: Mother?

M: Theresa May, Prime Minister of the United Kingdom.

T: Mother?

M: Is your mother with you?

T: No . . . Are you my mother?

M: No, I'm *not* your mother, though our countries *do* share a special relationship.

T: Okay, don't get freaky. Listen. I'm calling you today because we need to establish normalization of diplomatic relations with our nations. We have been enemies for too long. It is time for the war to end.

M: There is no war between the United States and the United Kingdom, Mr. Trump—

T: Excuse me.

M: Mr. President, I—

T: Excuse me.

M: Mr. President, I—

T: Excuse me.

M: Mr. President, I—

T: Excuse me.

M: Mr. President—

T: There was a war, and we won it. And you're not going to tell me any different.

M: There was a war after that war that we won.

T: Paul Retard rode through the streets with his lantern giving Christmas presents to everybody.

M: Yes, and then in the War of 1812 we burned down the White House.

T: What?!

M: Dolly Madison escaped with the papers and paintings.

T: She was a sheep that could talk like a woman!

M: Very well. Mr. President—

T: Yes?

M: Mr. President, I must lodge my objection to your posting on Twitter inciteful racialist propaganda from the UK's far right party.

T: I don't know what it was. It was a tweet, I like to tweet. I sent the tweet out, it was a guy, a Muslim guy beating someone up. How can you beat that? And I didn't know what it was from, from the right or whatever. Who can tell what your parties are like, anyway? You don't have a Democrat and a Republican. What am I supposed to do? So I put it out. But if it offended anybody, then I'm sorry that it offended anyone, but that's the most I'm gonna say. And the truth is, I agree with the video. And isn't your hard right basically a liberal Democrat anyway?

M: They're an anti-Muslim, anti-immigrant, nationalist isolationist party.

T: There you go, that's my kind of party, baby. You like to party?

M: No. Mr. President—

T: Where's the queen?

M: The queen is in Windsor Castle.

T: Wow!

M: I'm not really supposed to say that. I'm not supposed to say where she is at any given moment, but I do know.

T: Why aren't I talking to her? Isn't she the head of state?

M: Yes, she's the figurehead head of state, I'm the head of the government.

T: She's the queen!

M: That's right.

T: And I only talk to the top. Get the queen on the phone.

M: I'll try . . . I'm afraid she's unavailable.

T: You didn't try!

M: I did try!

T: How could you do that that quick?

M: I have an assistant.

T: Who? Is she hot?

M: His name is Daniel.

T: Oh, I see, those guys, they know how to pick out good ties. I don't have a problem with them, okay? They know how to organize things.

M: Certainly. Now, regarding your state visit to the United Kingdom—

T: Oh, boy!

M:—to London—

T: I can't wait! I'm gonna go see all the big sights. I want to see the Buckingham Castle and I want to go to the big wheel, and I'm gonna see the knights, and I wanna go see the Battle of Hasty Pudding, and all the good times. And I wanna ride in a carriage like a queen!

M: Well, Mr. President, it is with great regret that I must inform you that your invitation has been rescinded.

T: Those guys with the furry hats in front of the castle, is that their hair or hats?

M: It's a hat.

T: Really? They could grow a lot of hair real big like that.

M: Perhaps.

T: You'd save money on the hats.

M: Perhaps.

T: Per hats?! Per hats, it's gotta cost what, twelve cents per hat? You save that money with the hair, you're talking twelve cents' savings. How many soldiers you got, what, five hundred soldiers?

M: I will be sure to take these suggestions under advisement, but I do—

T: Where's your husband?

M: My husband is a banker and is not in public life. Now I frankly must insist that you acknowledge that your invitation has been rescinded.

T: What?! Excuse me, no one disinvites Donald Trump from anywhere. I'm taking my plane and I'm landing it in the Heath. I take rescinded for my sciatica! Its side effects are dementia, loss of sight, inability to have orgasms without having fast food in the bed with you, not wanting to talk to your wife, having the hots for your daughter . . .

M: Very well, I'm afraid I have other business to tend to today.

T: What could you possibly have to do?

M: I'll send your regards to Her Majesty the queen.

T: Get her on the phone.

M: I can't.

T: Get the queen mother on the phone.

M: I can't. She passed on—

T: Where?

M:—years ago.

T: Did she take the rainbow bridge?

M: Pardon?

T: Rainbow bridge, when everyone dies they walk on and they go to another magic place.

M: Ah, yes. I'm not familiar with your cosmology. I suppose so.

T: I don't wear makeup. Daniel, connect me to the queen, that's an order!

M: What?

T: Your assistant is our spy. Now, Daniel!

(EU Phone ring)

Queen Elizabeth II: Hello?

T: Hello?

Q: Who is this?

T: This is Donald Trump, president of the United States. You're the queen, right?

Q: That's correct.

T: Wow! You're in Windsor Castle, huh?

Q: Yes.

T: Listen, I don't want your middle management talking to me anymore. That Theresa May's a real drag.

Q: Oh, yes, well I suppose opinions differ.

T: We can negotiate a deal right now. First off, I want the British troops out of the United States. Your occupation ends today.

Q: Very well . . .

T: I won the war!

CALL: RODRIGO DUTERTE, PRESIDENT OF THE
PHILIPPINES

Trump: Okay, it's ringing . . .
Duterte: Hello, Mr. President.

(two gunshots ring out)

T: What's that?
D: Another drug dealer trying to pollute our children's minds and sell his junk on the street.
T: Wow, you scaring him with firecrackers?
D: That's right, I threw firecrackers out the window and it makes them disperse so they can be summarily executed by my soldiers around the corner.
T: So wonderful. I wish we could Sumerian execute people. Because in Sumeria, they knew how to do it. That was ancient, right?
D: I don't know, sir. I'm living for the present.
T: You're living for me?!
D: The present, sir.
T: Where?
D: I live in the Philippines. I'm told you're calling to congratulate me.
T: Congratulations on an incredible victory. You beat Hillary Clinton. She ran to the Philippines to try to take some of that Corazon Aquino heat. As we all know, you beat Corazon Aquino, the Filipino Hillary Clinton, to become the president of the Philippine United States. It was an incredible victory. But I have to say, what you're doing over there, very good, very tough. You gotta be tough on the drugs, and the

drug dealers, and make sure these people get paid. I wish we could do a little of what you do over there.

D: Well, it's easy, sir. All you have to do is send some soldiers out to indiscriminately kill civilians.

T: I don't know how we could do that here. It's much more tough. Much more tough. But I like what you're doing, because the drugs are very bad. My brother died of a terrible drug and drinking problem. You woulda killed him! You woulda gotten him first and taught him a lesson: You're dead! But I'm calling you today to once again say the Filipino—you're a great people. You're China without being China. You're American China. You're like a sideways China. Cause we all know the great Joseph McCarthy—that was the guy, right? When Roy Cone sent Joseph McCarthy over to get all the Communists out of the Philippines, they said, "Old soldiers never give up, they just Faye Dunaway." Anyway, how's it going over there? Is it hot?

D: Yes, it's always hot, sir. It's a tropical archipelago.

T: Well I don't know specifically what island it is, but I can tell you this: I love it so much. It's actually 75 degrees here today. It's very nice. Philippines! You've gotta make the better deal. We know that you people export so many coconuts. All the coconuts. And when Gilligan and his crew landed on your island, they built your nation out of nothing. The Professor, Mary Ann, Thurston Howell the Third, all contributed to what makes the Philippines Island great. Philippines Island. Where the Professor, Mary Ann, and all the greats . . . You guys still have the Harlem Globetrotters over there?

D: Uh, no sir.

T: What happened?

D: I don't know, sir. We were talking about drug policy, weren't we?

T: We need to deal with the drugs. Over here we're working on creating better enforcement for drug policy. So much of it comes from Mexico. What's your Mexico?

D: It's the north of our own country, sir. We've got rebels up there, active rebellion.

T: Your Mexico's upside down? Your China's sideways, and your Mexico's upside down. It's very strange on your side of the world. What is it, Saturday over there? Let me tell you something, I hear when you go under the Equator, the toilets spray everything out! See, here in America when you flush the toilet, it goes in the hole. But I hear over in Philippines, it blows it out! . . . Hello? Hello. I think we got disconnected.

(shots ring out)

T: What's going on?!

D: More firecrackers, sir.

T: Why don't we have firecrackers, Kelsey?

Kelsey: I'll ask around, sir.

T: No, don't, I'm scared!

INTERVIEW: MELANIA TRUMP, FIRST LADY

Kelsey: It's so nice to speak to you on the eve of what is going to be perhaps your most visible official act as First Lady, your first state dinner.

Melania: Yes, I am very proud to share our first dinner with the Macrons of France. I am inspired by the history that our countries share . . .

T: What's going on in here? Who are you talking to? Is there a guy in here?

K: It's Kelsey, sir, I'm talking to Melania. Mrs. Trump.

T: In the map room? Why the map room? Is she showing you the route her shipping container took? Oh great, here we go, she's giving me the look. It's funny!

K: We're talking about the state dinner with France tomorrow evening.

M: Yes, it will be a more intimate affair than some of the larger parties of past presidents.

T: Intimate affair, what do you know about those? Either of you?

M: I mean that other presidents threw bigger parties.

T: Who? Who?

M: I won't say.

T: Who? Who threw a big party?

M: Obama. Obama threw a big party.

T: You bitch, you said the name!

M: You asked! You asked me to say!

K: That's right, the Obama administration's last state dinner was in a tent on the white house lawn for the Italian prime minister, and there were almost four hundred people in attendance.

T: Shut up, shut up about that. Is that what he talked to you about? Is that what you were laughing about?

M: Laughing? What laughing?

T: At Babby Bushie's! I saw you laughing and talking, you and Barack at Babbie Bushe's. Tell me, tell me what you said to him.

M: I said nothing! I said I like his wife's clothes.

T: Don't you lie to me. Don't you lie. Is he throwing you a party in some tent somewhere? Trash. You're both trash. We'll have a bigger tent. More people. Call the guy. We're getting a tent and more people and you won't be there.

K: Your menu choices seem like they're original but unpretentious.

M: Don't ruin this! Why do you ruin this? This could be best . . .

T: Be best? Be best? Listen to yourself. I'll throw the party. You won't be there. You're out. Get out. This is over. Get out.

M: You ruin this, you make everything so sad!

T: Get out! Hopey and I are coming in for a talk and a rub. Get out. Map room is for the president. That's an order.

TRANSCRIPT: ELON MUSK MEETING

Trump: I can smell you from a mile away.

Musk: Excuse me?

T: Musk. I can smell your presence.

M: Sir, I thought you'd be sitting at the desk of the Oval Office, not lurking in the corner over there.

T: No.

M: I was warned about this—you like to watch people come in the door.

T: I like to peer. All day I peer out the windows of the Oval Office going, "Who's that?! Who's that on the lawn? Who's that! Are those kids skateboarding? Get 'em out of here!"

M: Well, I'm sorry to say I have to leave your business council.

T: What?!

M: I have to leave, sir. I strongly disagree with your immigration ban. And I can't believe you're considering introducing tariffs on aluminum or other raw materials. I think it's going to be a disaster for the American economy.

T: Listen to me, trust me. We're not going to really do a ban. That's just for my base. I'm gonna tell them this was the best that we could do. As long as I support law enforcement and we have enough film of black kids getting shot in the street and Latinos getting locked up, then we'll be fine. Trust me. I mean, who's gonna make your super Tesla car if you don't have immigrants? You car guys. Hot rod boys. That's what you do, right? Hot rods?

M: I also run a private space program.

T: Like *I Dream of Jeannie*?

M: I'm sorry?

T: Larry Hagman from *I Dream of Jeannie*. Lieutenant Nelson?

M: Oh, right.

T: He went up into space?

M: He was an astronaut on the show, and the genie came from space.

T: No, Jeannie didn't come from space.

M: She didn't?

T: He went up in the cartoon. God. I can't believe this. You didn't watch the opening cartoon of *I Dream of Jeannie*? He goes up into space and then he comes back to Earth, but his capsule lands on a deserted island. And there on the island he finds a genie bottle and he rubs it and out pops a hot genie in a genie outfit.

M: That's funny, I always thought she came from space, it was actually a big inspiration for me.

T: It's Barbara Eden! She comes from a bottle!

M: I thought it was space.

T: How could the bottle be space?

M: I thought the bottle was out in space.

T: No, it was never out in space. It was always on the island.

M: I must have skimmed the cartoon.

T: Skimmed the cartoon, are you kidding me? What is this guy talking about. The cartoon! Barbara Eden. The genie she gets brought back to the apartment, but her magic powers are a little thrown off because, like, she's been trapped in the bottle for so long. So she's always trying to help her master, you know? And that's the way it should be. I tell Melania to call me master. Okay?

M: Will the First Lady be by? I was looking forward to meeting her.

T: No, Melania's at a Best Western in Arlington.

M: I see.

T: That's what she told me. She said, "That's it!" Oh, it was another one of those nights. Let me tell ya. I almost gave her another kidney problem. So, we go up to the residence, right? Which is terrible, it's so gross up there. The Obamas made this weird kitchen. It's so stupid. There's not just a hot plate. That's how I know how to heat up food. And I go upstairs, and I've been working like, for four hours. So I go upstairs, and it's almost time for *Hardball*. And I gotta watch *Hardball* because then I go to Fox, and I see what they say, and after Fox I go to CNN to watch Don Lemon, but then oh boy, wait a minute, Judge Judy reruns at ten! So then I gotta watch Judge Judy on WTTG, that's My9 in New York, which I get piped down here. That gets me to eleven, and then it's time for *The 11th Hour with Brian Williams*, which makes no sense. Why's it called *The 11th Hour*? It's the twenty-third hour of the day! And while I was trying to tell Melania how much this was getting under my skin, I get the same old same old from her. "Everything you say is nonsense! I am so unhappy! You are my curse, you are my curse!" And she stormed out, so then I called Hannity and he told me what's wrong with my wife.

M: Sir, while I have you, I also wanted to discuss the issue of protectionist federal and state regulation precluding Tesla selling cars directly on the Internet.

T: We're gonna fix that. We're gonna fix direct cars on the Internet. Sell it on the Internet. We'll fix all of that. Whatever states you need, the states that don't buy the cars, we're gonna buy the cars. We're gonna advertise them and make sure that the cars are sold.

M: Perhaps we could streamline some of the—

T: I wanna go to space!

M: I'm sorry, sir?

T: I wanna go to space.

M: Well, we're not sending people to space yet. We just sent that rocket up.

T: You sent that guy up in that car! Don't lie to me!

M: He's not a guy, sir, he's a mannequin.

T: He's driving to space!

M: It's a mannequin, sir. There's no man there.

T: It was so cool. You ever see *Heavy Metal*?

M: I think I did at some point, sir.

T: It's an animation tour de force. Where different rock bands play along to different animations. And they're so cool. And one of them, a car drives in space! And that's what you did!

M: That's true, sir.

T: Where's that space man driving to, anyway?

M: Well, I guess eventually he'll burn up in the sun.

T: Let's get to the real business at hand. Kelsey, don't listen to this, close your ears, go take a walk.

K: Yes sir.

T: The real business, Musk. The time window is closing. The one my uncle opened. The multiverse oscillator in the Hotel New Yorker is no longer dependable. I understand Nikola had more secret documents. I'm hoping I can get them translated in time to augment the window so I can pierce the firmament and gain access to a deeper layer of alternate realities.

M: Sir, my people are working as hard as they can. But the code is unbreakable.

T: Listen to me. My uncle didn't take on Nikola Tesla's papers, translate them, and then give them to you so you could start a stupid car company and a space flight center that sends dummies into space in hot cool cars like it's the cover of a J. Geils Band album! I wanna go to space!

M: We're working as fast as we can.

T: Build the time window. Complete it. Stabilize it. That is all. Also, I need to find a parallel universe where Ivanka and I aren't directly related.

M: Sir, that's not how multiverse transitioning works.

T: Oh, come on. What are you talking about?

M: The closest you could get would be an adjacent universe where everything's the same except one day you did something slightly different.

T: Like what?

M: Like you decided to take the stairs instead of the elevator.

T: Well that'll never happen. Not unless the prime bannister of England's there. Theresa May, Mother May I. Tell that Space Man I love him.

M: He knows, sir.

T: He knoooows. Come in major mannequin, can you hear me talking to you . . .

M: Actually we played *Starman*.

DECISION-MAKING DECISIONS

A president's most important job is to decide to make the decisions that no one else could decide. Below is the process President Trump used to make his decision to decide to bomb Syria after Bashar al-Assad used chemical weapons against his own people.

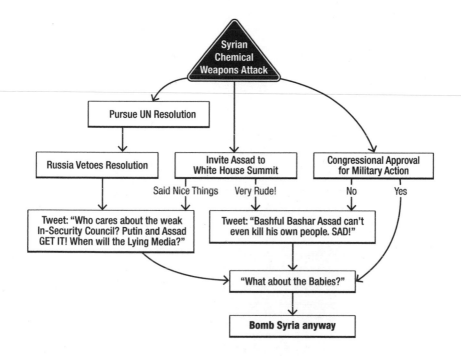

THE SECRET LOT

THE WAIT IS OVER FOR MORE JACK RENEGADE! NOW AVAILABLE IN PAPERBACK: STEVE BANNON'S TALE OF CASTING COUCHES AND CORRUPT CARDINALS BEHIND THE "SCENES" IN HOLLYWOOD: **THE SECRET LOT!**

THE SECRET LOT

We all know that the sons of Abraham and the sons of Shem are in eternal schism. The true sons of Abraham are the Semitic people of the Middle East, whereas the sons of Ashkezar bear false witness to the God of the Mountain. In truth, they have always been scriveners who pervert the ancient rites and rituals which then become offensive to the sight of the Almighty. As the Ashkenazi moved through Europe and eventually set sail from the continent, they settled on the East Coast of the United States. Unable to earn an honest living, they moved west and made camp in an area that felt familiar to them: the arid desert of Los Angeles, a city of angels ready for the fall. Having smuggled the technology they stole from Thomas Edison to where the long arm of the patent office could not reach, they settled down and built new temples: Metro Goldwyn Mayer, Columbia, Paramount, and Universal, where they worshipped the Luciferian light and created mechanisms for its amplification and export. They built a fortified citadel of propaganda to dispatch new golden calves each week to every town and then every home from sea to shining sea.

———————————

Jack Renegade peeled his back off the leather sofa with a fart, grimacing at the young starlet unsatisfied with the mashings of his weak member that never fully engorged. "Get back to the casting line." She smiled, more than a little embarrassed. He could sense that she knew he was okay. And she was okay, too, since she would get what she really wanted from the encounter after he made a few calls. Then maybe she'd be waiting for him in a Star Wagon later that week, if he could find her. It was a little game they played. Jack Renegade pulled up his khakis, buttoned them, threw on a polo, a shirt, and a jacket over that. "Don't be late for your screen test. I'll call you tomorrow." What was an Oxford-educated symbologist doing working in the slums of Hollywood backlots? Jack thought. His father was in the Navy when he was the same age Jack was today. Everything was artificial here, not like the sea.

The door slammed shut behind Jack as he entered his home office off his living room. It was time to get to work. He pushed aside a telescript about a Jewish comic living in New York with his three friends. He didn't care to review it right now, because he had deeper work to do. "Goddamn my ex-wife for even putting this script in front of me." Still, he missed her. She was still closing down that property with the hot tub filled with acid in Florida. Not all the memories were bad.

"Snap out of it," Jack said to himself. He wasn't here just to soil starlets and argue with studios over production rights. That was just the cover. The University of British London had commissioned him to travel across the pond once again for a much deeper mission in Los Angeles. Renegade was familiar with Tinseltown; he had been there before, even dabbled in the business. It was child's play compared to the ancient symbols and manuscripts from lost civilizations he'd made a career of discovering and translating on a daily basis. But here he was, right in the heart of the beast. The devilish Jew runs this town. Renegade knew they weren't all bad, he had plenty of Jewish friends! But he also knew how they operated. "A white man can't get a job in this business anymore," Renegade said to himself, dumping a jar of change into a bag for the bank. Now was the time to get what was his. And he had just the plan to do it.

Renegade kicked open the doors to Lou Rubenstein's casting office. The secretary stood up and said, "Sign in here. Do you need sides?"

"Yes, of course I do. I'm not prepared for this audition."

But Renegade was totally prepared. He had found the entrance to the secret lot, the place where all the movies are truly made, and the dark Kabbalah magic that's practiced in order to reprogram the minds of the American people to support a Judaic political agenda. All he had to do was nail this session. If he booked the job, he'd be in the secret lot before he knew it.

The show was called *Seinfeld*. He was reading for the part of a soup salesman that was really tough. Renegade waited his turn, read the sides, the door opened, and there he saw the casting director, his haggard, sunken features attesting to the centuries of inbreeding that had brought him here to stand behind the little tripod. Renegade knew how to play this game.

"Hi, uh, Jack Renegade, reading for Paul? All right, no soup for you. No soup for you." He didn't like that one; his mouth was a little dry. "Do you mind if I do that again? Can you give me just a moment, I'm sorry." Renegade went out in the hallway. He was sweating bullets. Truth was, he wished he had prepared for this. Even just a little bit. He was always a self-saboteur, even at the University of British London. But he had to get in that lot. "No soup for you. No soup for *you*. *NO* soup for you."

Later that night, another thousand-dollar call girl made her way out of Renegade's room at the Hollywood Hawaiian hotel chuckling to herself. As the clock struck nine, Renegade finally tensed in ecstacy. She had been gone five minutes when he was able to dribble something onto the pillowcase. He rolled over and said quietly "Well, I did it. She was here at one point."

His phone rang. It was his agent. "What happened today?"

"What do you mean? I thought I did a great job. They loved me!"

"Well, they don't want you. They're passing."

"What?! You're kidding me. Goddamnit! Olivia, I gotta get in there. You don't understand. Ask them to see me again. Please. Tell them I'll read for anything."

After months of auditioning, Jack decided to purchase the rights to *Seinfeld* instead. He had to part with his Eye of Horus for a trunkful of Spanish bullion that arrived six days late by UPS Ground, but it was good business. Jack now was a part owner of *a hit show*, including its residual rights, which gave him access to the most secret temple: The Chateau Marmont. Three knocks at the valet stand and a whispered riddle to the hostess would get him whisked to the best seat in the house most nights if he avoided the really busy times. On Wednesday, Jack was finishing a delicious hamburger there and he saw none other than Matt Weiner from *Mad Men*. He was too scared to approach him— you can't just go up to someone without having a project or a deal in hand— but Renegade wasn't intimidated. So he ordered a glass of champagne and placed a silver token of St. Theodore among the bubbles and had it sent over to Weiner's table. But he forgot to indicate who it was from, so Weiner just looked confused and told the waitress to send it away.

Renegade was dejected. That night, he drove up to the valley. He thought maybe he would pick a fight with some Mexican teenagers in the parking lot of a 7-Eleven or just get an egg salad sandwich there since he was tired. Before he made up his mind, Jack's agent called again.

"You booked it!"

"The Bounty paper towel commercial?"

"You know it, buddy!"

Now Jack had a direct flight to the Second Sphere. He called his contact at the Vatican collect and left a quick little message after the beep when he was supposed to say his name: "Our plan will have to wait."

Archivist's Note

Never in human history has a man accomplished so much in so short a time as the Donald J. Trump in the first year of his presidency. One by one we announced these words at the beginning of each day, and again when regrouping after our leader's afternoon sugar nap. But it was not a platitude. Donald Trump had delivered on all his campaign promises: Tax Reform favoring Job Creators. Dismantling ObamaCare through the back door. Jettisoning the Iran Deal. Tough talk with North Korea. Diplomacy with Russia. Making our NATO Allies pay their fair share for their own defense. And of course the biggest win for the outsider businessman genius who ascended to the highest office in the world: The nomination of not one, but two justices to the Supreme Court. One of the new justices was even willing to read a press release that the president personally wrote for him. How's that for vertical integration?

The mood in the inner circle was ecstatic, especially once the president cast off the remaining deadweight. Every so often there would be a little office party at the end of the day, and I was honored to be invited since it kept me at the office and away from the mini-bar. Pruitt would bring a massage chair. Justice Kennedy would stop by. Steve

Mnuchin would bring booze by the case, and his charming, beautiful wife took selfies with everyone. The brass from ICE were always sniffing around for an invitation so they could remind the president personally that they felt they reported directly to him. At the last get-together, Stephen Miller played an "auto-tuned" dubstep remix he made of the audio from the immigrant detention center that was in the news that week. It was in bad taste, sure, but you had to admit it was funny, and actually pretty catchy!

WINNING SICKNESS

TRANSCRIPT: REINCE PRIEBUS EXIT-INTERVIEW

Trump: Come on in. Come on in. Can you believe we're on a plane?

Priebus: Yes sir.

T: It feels like an office.

P: Yes sir.

T: Look at this. Look at that stain on the sofa. Who do you think made that?

P: Well, I assume it was you, sir. You have a similar stain on your pants.

T: This is why you're going. Because it's not me—

P: I understand, sir.

T: Stephen Miller dropped a crème brûlée on the sofa.

P: Very well, sir.

T: It was so delicious, Reince. So good. Well—

P: Mr. President, it has been my honor to serve you—

T: Okay, all right.

P: The 45th president of the United States—

T: Okay, Reince.

P: And to work at this White House, a lifelong dream.

T: Yeah yeah yeah. Did I just fire you?

P: Yes sir. And now, I'll be going.

T: What?

P: I'll take my leave, sir.

T: Wait a minute.

P: I'll fly home commercial and I'll find my way back.

T: Hold on. First off, we've gotta do something called an exit inter-view. It's done in all great businesses, and we also did it at Trump International, and we're gonna do it now. Now sit down and be care-ful, make sure you put your seat belt on, because even though we're on the ground, there still could be some turbulence. You got the seat belt on?

P: Yes sir.

T: Now, Reince.

P: Hold on, I gotta tighten it.

T: Reince, you did an incredible job being a worm. Everybody knows that you're a total sleazebag. The only reason I took you on is because I wanted to make sure the Republican party had no way to void me out of the system as soon as I got the nomination. And you know that, and I know that.

P: Yes sir.

T: I wouldn't trust you as far as I could throw you.

P: Yes sir.

T: As far as I'm concerned, half the time when you leave, Melania goes, "Was there a slug in the yard?" And I go, "No, it was just Reince!"

P: Yes sir.

T: Your slime trail is so long and disgusting.

P: Can I offer you some feedback, sir?

T: This is an exit interview!

P: Yes, but, uh, customarily in an exit interview I can comment on my experiences with the company. Can I?

T: This is very true, Reince, but keep it quick, because I got two Fish Filets, a BK Broiler and Double-Double, Animal Style from In-N-Out being driven in from Nevada—

P: I know, sir. I placed the order.

T: I know you did. And I hope you got it right. I hope—and I'm checking all that food for spit, because I know how it works when you fire people. They spit in your food and they leave upper deckers in your toilets, and I'm not having any of that.

P: I'm not going to do that, sir.

T: Well, then who left that upper decker in the toilet?

P: I assume it was you, sir, because you said, "I'm gonna leave an upper decker in the airplane toilet."

T: That's right! It was me!

P: Sir, before I leave, I want to ask you to please start showing up to work before eleven o'clock in the morning.

T: I'm at work. I'm in the White House.

P: Yes, sir, I know. Well, we're on Air Force One right now.

T: Right. That's the White House in the air. Wherever I am is the White House.

P: That's not true, sir.

T: And whenever I wake up is when the White House starts working.

P: That's not true, sir. Most of us start working around six.

T: Whoa.

P: We wait for you for about five hours. Our day is half done by the time you roll into the Oval.

T: Well, first off, the bed's very uncomfortable here. The pillows are too plush.

P: That's productive, sir. We can do something about that.

T: And nobody goes in the bed except me. Not even Melania, okay? I'm the one who takes care of the bed. And my problem is, I don't get a good sleep. I stay up, I watch the *Red Eye*—I love *Red Eye*. You ever seen *Red Eye* on Fox?

P: I've seen it.

T: I watch the *Red Eye* and then I go to sleep. And it's like 2:30 in the morning, I gotta get nine hours. You're supposed to get nine hours a night. So then, two o'clock to ten, eleven—that's nine hours! Get him out!

P: Very well, sir. It's been an honor to—

T: Get him out of here!

P: It's been an honor, sir.

T: Get him out of here, folks.

P: Goodbye, sir.

T: Out!

P: I'm going, sir.

T: Reince? Reince. Get him back in.

[jet engines drown out audio]

T: Stop the jet! Stop the jet. Hold on.

P: Yes sir?

T: Get back on here.

P: Yes sir.

T: Turn the plane off. Get in here, sit down. We haven't finished, I've decided.

P: You asked me to leave, sir.

T: I said get him out because I didn't like what you were saying.

P: I was encouraging you to spend a little less time in bed.

T: Encouragement. I don't like encouragement.

P: Okay, sir.

T: How about suggestionment? Okay? Suggestionment. And then you can give me a little mint. Just give me a suggestion, and give me a mint. Say, "Why don't you wake up a little earlier. Here's a mint!" And then maybe I'll listen to you.

P: If you think that would work, sir, I will come back tomorrow with some mints.

T: No! What, you think my breath stinks? Get out of here! I don't have stinky breath! Get him out of here!

P: Yes sir.

T: Get him out!

P: Yes sir.

T: And beat him up on the way out, I'll give you fifty bucks. I'll cover your legal fees! Beat him up! Throw him down the stairs!

P: Ouch! They gave me a little nudge, sir.

T: Hey, what are you, Secret Service?

Secret Service: Yes sir.

T: Where's Reince?

SS: He just walked down the steps, sir, to the tarmac.

T: Are we leaving?

SS: We were planning to, sir.

T: Oh, wait! I gotta ask Reince some other questions before he goes! Get him back!

SS: He's gone, sir, he's walking away—he's crossing a taxiway, sir.

T: Drive the plane up to him. Scoop him up. Scoop him up with the wheel well. Put him in the wheel well like a Nigerian.

SS: He's running, sir.

T: Chase him down!

T: Get in here.

P: Yes sir.

T: I'm not done with you yet.

P: I just ruffled my suit a little, sir.

T: Well, that's fine. Ruffles have ridges, everybody knows that. Ruffles pick up more dip than other chips, do you know that?

P: Surface area.

T: Of course! And here's the thing: I don't eat a Pringle, and I don't trust people who eat Pringles. It's compressed potato powder. Who's ever heard of eating compressed dry mashed potato powder?

P: I don't know, sir.

T: And also, a Ruffle always goes with any dip. I have a few questions before you go.

T: Who's taking over for you?

P: I don't know.

T: You're supposed to find a replacement before you go!

P: If you'd like me to do that before I leave, it will take me a couple of weeks, sir.

T: No, forget it, I don't want you around for a couple of weeks.

P: All right, sir.

T: No, don't leave!

P: Okay.

T: The papers I get in the morning. Who's gonna read them to me? The thing about the Russians and the Chinese and the big Iran thing.

P: The presidential daily brief?

T: I don't know.

P: You could get Pompeo, or really anyone in your cabinet.

T: I don't trust them, they're too volcanic. I try to talk to any of them and the next thing you know I'm screaming.

P: Well, sir, you're going to have to solve some of those problems on your own.

T: No, I'm sorry. Your job, before you leave, is to solve all the problems and leave everything up to speed.

P: That's going to take a little while, sir. That's what I've been trying to do.

T: Don't you forget that you know what I know about Russia, don't you forget it. You know what I know, and I'll take you out. You hear me?

P: Yes sir.

T: You think you can bury yourself, you little earthworm? Okay? There was a book about kids who ate worms, okay, and I'm the biggest kid and I eat all the worms and I don't care what you say, okay? And, let me tell you something. It's your fault.

P: Sir, my phone is telling me that my Uber has arrived and I've—

T: They don't let Ubers come to the airport tarmac, stop lying to me!

P: It's just outside the gate.

T: Well, then it can wait. And if it doesn't—

P: I'm paying by the minute.

T: Well good.

P: I got myself an Uber Pool, which means there's probably other people waiting in it too.

T: Jesus, Reince. What was your life like before you joined this administration?

P: Do you really want to know, sir?

T: Yes.

P: Well sir, I—

T: Get him out of here! Get him out! Bye-bye, don't let the jet engine hit you on the ass on the way out!

T: Pilot, take us into the air. Second star to the right, and straight on till morning!

Pilot: Yes, sir, back to Washington, DC.

T: Whatever!

CALL: AREA 51

Trump: What if an alien picks up?

Colonel Monroe: Sir, yes, hello. This is Colonel Monroe—

T: Colonel Monroe!

C: Sir, yes, sir.

T: Sir, yes, sir.

C: Yes sir, this is Colonel Monroe. I am the Operations Director of Area 51, how can I help you?

T: I didn't know if you were playing a word game with me.

C: No sir.

T: Good for you, soldier. You're a tough guy, I can tell through the phone.

C: Yes sir.

T: We were sitting here in the Oval Office. I've been having many discussions about the secrets that the government keeps from the American people.

C: I am not at liberty to discuss classified matters over this line, sir, especially if there are other people present.

T: No, it's— I can talk to you, I'm the president! This is the most classified line and most classy line that's ever existed.

C: Yes sir.

T: And can I also tell you, excuse me, can I also tell you, the only people in the room besides me are Ivanka, Jared, General McMaster, two Russian diplomats, and three other guys I don't know. And my Jewish granddaughters, but they're playing on the floor. Bubby and Zadie.

C: Isn't that what they call you, sir?

T: Huh?

C: Isn't that what they call you, sir?

T: Well, when Melania and I see them, they say, "Bubby, Zadie!" because that must be their names.

C: Very well, sir. I've made a note of the people on the call.

T: Anyway, America—for too long, our secrets have been secret. They've been locked away from the discerning eye, from the incredible American eyes of my voters and supporters. Part of making America great again is also bringing into the light. It's time to reveal the secrets of Area 51. So, let's dish! Tell me what's going on over there.

C: Sir, unless you're willing to declassify documents unilaterally, which would have to be done by executive order, I'm not at liberty to discuss any secret, top secret, or otherwise classified material on this line in the company that you're keeping, sir.

T: Executive order: Tell me your secrets.

C: Sir, I'm afraid I'm going to have to see the paperwork behind that order, sir. With all due respect.

T: It's right here. I'm looking at it.

C: I have to see it. Sir. Then, if you want to inspect any classified material, that is your right.

T: As an American.

C: No, as the president of the United States, sir, it is your right to inspect any classified material, and I'm sure you could arrange transportation to Area 51 at your convenience, sir.

T: How do I get there?

C: It's in Nevada, sir.

T: All right, let's start with the simple ones. Where are the aliens? I know there's an alien street, alien tourists visit Area 51, which is unbelievable that Americans can't go visit Area 51 but you're letting illegal aliens from space go visit it—

C: I assure you we're not, sir.

T: Where are the alien bodies kept?

C: We don't have any alien bodies, sir. And if we did I would not be at liberty to discuss them on this line.

T: There you go again, there you go again "and if we"—why do you say that?!

C: Sir, if you order me to answer honestly, I'll have to resign.

T: Oh man! Okay. We'll do this another way. How's this: we'll play twenty questions. Ready? Twenty questions.

C: I'll answer as many questions as you like, sir.

T: No, twenty—don't you know the game twenty questions?

C: I've heard of it, sir.

T: What do you mean, you've heard of it?

C: I've heard of it, sir. I've never played.

T: You've never played twenty questions?

C: I've never played it to my knowledge, sir, but I'm familiar with it as a game.

T: Oh my god.

C: I've never played pinochle either, but I'm aware of it.

T: You know what, you'd be terrible at a party, you know that?

C: That's why I don't go to many parties, sir. I take my life very seriously.

T: Fine. Twenty questions. I'm going to ask you something—think of something secret at Area 51.

C: Very well, sir.

T: Is it an animal, vegetable, or mineral?

C: None of those, sir.

T: What do you mean, neither?

C: It's a number.

T: Okay . . .

C: I'm thinking of a secret number.

T: Secret number . . . is it high?

C: Compared to what, sir?

T: No! It's gotta be yes or no!

C: Yes.

T: High number. That's one down. Okay. Is it a round number?

C: Yes sir.

T: Does it have an 8 in it?

C: No sir.

T: Does it have a 3 in it.

C: No sir.

T: Does it have a 0 in it?

C: Yes sir.

T: Whoa. How many— Oh . . . are the total number of numbers higher than 6?

C: No.

T: Oooh. Is it 000?

C: No.

T: 001.

C: No.

T: 002?

C: No.

T: Is it three numbers?

C: No.

T: Four?

C: No.

T: Two.

C: Yes.

T: 00.

C: No.

T: Is the other number—

C: I already said it's an even number, sir. Zero's not even or odd, it's zero.

T: Is it 10?

C: No.

T: 20.

C: Yes.

T: Whoa! Wow! And that's a secret number.

C: Yes, it's the code to the private bathroom in the officers' lounge.

T: Oh, come on, now! You gotta be kidding me. It's a two-digit code?

C: Well there are a lot of layers of security to get through before you can get anywhere near the officers' lounge here.

T: All right, fine. So. I want to know the secrets, Colonel. So what do I do to figure them out.

C: Well, you can come here, sir. We'll show you anything you like.

T: I gotta go there?

C: Yes sir.

T: I'm scared!

C: Sir, you can come here and I can show you absolutely anything about the base and should you choose to reveal it to the public, that is the prerogative of your office. But I cannot reveal any classified secret or top secret information without a written order declassifying that material.

T: No, I don't like to—I don't want to go out there.

C: We can show you everything, sir. We can show you the stuff downstairs.

T: Whoa, what do you mean downstairs?

C: I can't tell you, sir, but we have some interesting stuff downstairs, sir.

T: What's down there?

C: Well, we have several levels downstairs and if you went down there you'd see some interesting things.

T: Tell me one thing that's down there! I order you to tell me one thing!

C: Slimy guy.

T: What?! Wait a minute. There's a slimy guy?!

C: I'm not going to get into the details, sir, but there is a slimy creature. A slimy man.

T: Whoa, a slimy man. Is he slimy like uh—

C: I can't tell you more than that, sir.

T: Like Ted Cruz? Does he have a ship?

C: We have some interesting aircraft, sir.

T: Flying shaushers.

C: You mean saucers.

T: That's what I said, shaushers.

C: All I can say, sir, is that we have some interesting aircraft.

T: Are they round?

C: There's round parts, sir.

T: Ooooh! And the slimy guy fits in there?

C: I imagine he could, sir.

T: Oh! So he's the pilot of the spacecraft! Wait, hold on. Clear the room! I want everybody out of the Oval Office. Step step step step step. Door shut! Okay! I'm alone now. Now . . . this slimy guy. What's his deal?

C: Sir, I'm not at liberty to discuss any classified, secret, or top secret information on this line. I shouldn't have even—

T: Everybody left!

C: It doesn't matter, sir. I also doubt that that's the case.

T: What?!

C: I heard you say, "Step, step, door shut," sir, I didn't hear any rustling or movement. I imagine that your grandchildren would have wanted to say goodbye to you.

T: First off, you're wrong on that one. They love to run screaming from the room the second they're allowed. Second off, I order you to put the slimy guy on the phone.

C: You don't want to do that, sir.

T: Nothing I can do about it if I order you, so I'm ordering you. Put him on.

C: All right. Let him loose, boys!

(sounds of struggle, gurgling noises)

T: What's happening?!

(sticky noses, muffled "Slimy guy! Slimy guy!")

T: Whoa! What's happening over there?

(gunshots, screaming)

T: Get the slimy guy! Get him! Get him! Get him on the phone!

CALL: MAR-A-LAGO HOST STATION

Maître d': Hello, you've reached the dining room at Mar-a-Lago.

Trump: Is this the Maître d'? This is Donald J. Trump. I want to talk to the D.

M: Oh, hello sir. Yes, this is he.

T: Francesco, right?

M: That's right. Will you be visiting us this weekend, sir?

T: No, no, no. I'm not coming down—yeah, yeah, I'm coming down!

M: Very well, sir.

T: My wife's in the room. So I'm gonna say no, but when I say no, I mean yes. And when I say yes, I mean maybe. How's business?

M: Well, our second dinner service is going well tonight. We had a lot of 8:00 and 9:00 reservations, so the dining room is actually full now.

T: What was the table count tonight?

M: We had 94 tables with a total of 312 guests.

T: More four tops, six tops? Or we talking deuces?

M: Twos and fours, sir.

T: Ah, that's not good.

M: We had one six top earlier in the evening.

T: What's the matter with the big-party booking? I thought we made a whole new party package.

M: Well, we did, sir, but it's the off season.

T: I don't care. We should be getting fifteen, twenty. People coming in from the rain, people coming in from the thunderstorms. Are you pushing the salad? We've got that great house salad.

M: We're always pushing the salad, sir—

T: That house salad's one of the great house salads!

M: Well, we're in agreement there.

T: Mixed greens, diced red onion, delicious, fresh, vine ripened tomatoes, a sprinkle of feta. Pitted black olives—kalamata—kalamaTAAAA! And, of course, that raspberry vinaigrette.

M: Yes sir.

T: Are you telling everybody about it?

M: Yes, it's—

T: With your choice of sliced steak, grilled chicken, or seared tuna.

M: Yes sir. The waiters push the salad, sir.

T: Well, I don't think they're pushing it enough.

M: Well, sir, pushing the salad isn't going to get us six and eight tops into the restaurant. That's not going to book the party room.

T: You kidding me? It's all about the salad.

M: Sir, with all due respect, I'd think you'd want to be complaining to the marketing department and the sales department.

T: You're the maître d', right?

M: That's right.

T: Well, then you're the guy who's the face of the whole operation.

M: That's true, but they have to get in the door first.

T: Well, get them in the door.

M: That's not my job!

T: Maître d-d-d, ladida-da-doh, that's who you are. You're just singing to yourself, running around, are you sitting down? Are you sitting down at all?

M: Never, sir.

T: Never.

M: No sir.

T: I hope not.

M: No sir.

T: Is Adolfo—did he show up for his shift?

M: Adolfo's here, sir. He's in the back.

T: Tell those busboys they do a great job.

M: I'll pass that along, sir.

T: Listen. I want you to rustle up some business. Take a walk and take me with you. Put me on speakerphone, walk around the club.

M: I really shouldn't leave my station.

T: I'm the boss! And I'm the president. I'm your president and your boss. Go walk around with me! Are you walking?

M: Very well, sir. Yes, I'm walking. I'm about ten yards from the dining room.

T: Good. Walk right up to the first person who's not waiting to eat.

M: There's a woman here.

T: Put her on.

Female Customer: Hello?

T: Donald Trump here, on the phone. President of the United States.

FC: A man just handed me this phone.

T: I'm the president of the United States!

FC: Ah—yes sir. Well sir, let me stand up!

T: What?

FC: Hello!

T: Are you in a wheelchair?

FC: No, I was just sitting in one of the little rocking chairs on the veranda.

T: Well why don't you hustle your little ass into the delicious Mar-a-Lago restaurant?

FC: We ate there at seven.

T: What time is it now?

FC: Nine-thirty.

T: Well, time for second dinner! I have a second dinner.

FC: I'll . . . ask what my husband thinks.

T: Have you had the salad?

FC: Yes, I had the salad. It was delicious. There was red onion, a little tomato, a little bit of feta, kalamata olives—

T: Pitted?!

FC: I'm sorry?

T: They were pitted! The olives were, right?

FC: I believe so . . .

T: Wait a minute. Put the guy who handed you the phone on the line.

Maître d': Hello?

T: Are you guys pitting all the olives over there?

M: Well, they come pitted, sir. We buy them pitted.

T: You better check every hole. I expect you to check every pit hole before you put them in!

M: Well, sir, I'll tell the line cook—

T: I want you to personally do it, Francesco.

M: You want me to personally inspect every kalamata olive to be pitted?

T: I'm sorry, am I not making myself clear?

M: Sir, can I let this woman go, or do you want to talk to her again?

T: Grab her by the wrists.

M: I'm not going to do that, sir.

T: Miss?

M: Here you go, sir.

T: Are you going into dinner?

Female Customer: Hello? The man here seems very distraught.

T: What?

FC: The man who gave me the phone seems distraught, it seems like you told him some bad news.

T: I don't know. The guy's a real mope. Listen. Get in there, order a salad with seared tuna. You'll never regret it. And get the rolls with the butter for only five dollars more, and then we'll move on to appetizers. Or appeteasers, as I call 'em—because they tease your nipples and your tongue. They tease your nipples and your tongue and then you scissor with the appeteaser. Put your mouth back [tongue noises].

Male Customer: Excuse me, what are you saying to my wife? She put down the phone in disgust. It seems like everyone who talks to you on this phone gets upset and confused.

T: Oh, boy. That's just what I need, a lecture from you? Grab your wife by the wrist or the collarbone and thrust her into the Mar-a-Lago restaurant. You're having a second dinner! She told me she's still hungry.

MC: Is it on you?

T: No. What are you, nuts? I'm trying to drum up business.

MC: You want me to take my wife into the restaurant—the same restaurant we ate first dinner at—and pay for another meal?

T: You admit that there's a second dinner by saying "first." So now you're legally contracted to go in and eat another dinner, or I'll boot you out on this beach.

MC: I'm not contracted to any such thing.

T: We will expel you from your room, sir, if you don't have another dinner.

MC: Very well. I guess I'll just get that salad. It's delicious.

T: It's a wonderful salad.

TRANSCRIPT: STEVE BANNON EXIT INTERVIEW

Steve: You wanted to see me, sir?

Trump: Yeah. I do, Steve.

S: You know I don't usually take meetings when Ophiuchus is rising.

T: What do I look like, Nancy Reagan? I don't care. Steve, keep that stuff to yourself, all right? I only want to see the results.

S: Yes sir. Sir, I've been checking off some things on my white board that we've accomplished for you.

T: What are they? Tell me, Steve?

S: Well, so far the Supreme Court has upheld the immigration ban.

T: Gorsushh.

S: Yes, we have Neil Gorsuch is on the bench irritating the rest of the justices, which was our plan all along.

T: Yeah, he's such an annoying guy! We all knew that about him. Totally annoying guy, Gorsuch. His wife too. Two annoying people. "Oh did you see this, oh did you see this?" Always pointing things out! It's totally working! There's nothing like creating a government rash. Rash decisions! That's gonna be the musical you wanted to make, right Steve?

S: Yes sir.

T: I'm all for it. Consider me in. I love a good Broadway show. I always show up for the very beginning and then leave in the middle.

T: Listen, Steve, tell me about the Wolf.

S: Who?

T: That guy, the Michael Wolff guy. Goddamned Wolff! He used to stalk through the halls. I kept saying, "There's a wolf in here!" And everyone would go, "No, what the hell are you talking about." And I'd go, "Right there! There's a wolf!" And everyone said I was insane? Well, the wolf wrote a book!

S: Yes sir. We knew he was writing a book. You ordered us to give open interviews for the book.

T: Right. Sure. Belay that order!

S: You can't retroactively belay an order, sir.

T: I don't know. Listen to me. Yes you can. Let me tell you something. People are telling me what's in this book and it's not good for me. And it's not good for Don Jr., which is not good for me because we have the same name. You called him a Treasonaurus! How was my son meeting with the Russians treasonous? If they only knew! And I'm "unhinged"? Steve, you got a lot of 'splainin' to do! What is this, Steve? I go away for just a couple of nights to play at the Copacabana, and I come back to find you, Fred, and Ethel are doing something crazy!

S: I'm sorry, sir. I'll give another interview. I'll give a better interview.

T: No. You let me down, Steve. You let me down and you betrayed me. We're not supposed to let authors like this come into the White House and violate our sacred bond.

S: There's already one here, sir!

T: What, that guy?

S: Kelsey Nelson is here, sir, he's another one.

T: Excuse me.

S: He's been sitting here the whole time!

T: Kelsey Nelson is an old golf guy who always would tell me where the worst streams were, okay? Now, excuse me, Kelsey? You're writing a good book, aren't you?

K: Yes sir. You're going to love it.

T: Kelsey's writing a great book, okay? And that's the difference. I never heard the wolf say he was writing a good book, he'd just go "Hooooowwwwl" and run away into the night. You know, now I understand why there are so many headless goats on the White House lawn. Or was that you, Steve, sacrificing goats?

S: I'm not sacrificing them, sir. I'm doing ritual sex magic.

T: Oh, yeah, they're great! George Clinton played for them. And Bill Clinton too! George Clinton and Bill Clinton had a music baby named Chelsea Clinton. Lock up George Clinton. If George Clinton runs next, that's another Clinton I gotta deal with!

T: Kelsey is writing the big book everybody wants. He's building my library and the best part is, unlike in a real library, you can be as loud as you want when you're reading this book! My least favorite part about a book is that I can't talk when I'm reading it, except if it's a book on tape. Then I talk along with it! And I try to match the words. It's so easy. It always begins with "Once upon a time." Now, listen to me. I dealt with a lot of stuff from you. Steve, you introduced me to Ritual Sex Magic, the funk band. And I'll never forget that. And you've drawn runes all around the White House to ward off warlocks. I even took that walk with you to Washington's tomb because you said there was some magic light in there and that he was still alive and I could consult with him about presidential matters. And then we got in there and you tried to make a move on me! And I forgave you. But here's the point. Look at you. You're bloated, you're covered in psoriasis, you're flaking all over the place. You got too many shirts on, and I still took care of you.

S: I took care of *you*, sir.

T: Are you crying? Your eyes are watering.

S: I got you elected, sir.

T: Okay, your eyes are just watering. Excuse me, *I* got me elected, Steve. Your job was just to make sure that those whackjob tiki-torch-holding creeps and the David Dukes of the world would go along quietly, quietly, so we could execute our vision without anyone knowing about it. And now you go running your big mouth in the book? I bet you talked about that hot tub full of acid where you were making meth in that rental house in Florida!

S: Sir, what I'm hearing is that you think—

T: Pass me those nuts.

S: Here are the nuts, sir. What I'm hearing is that you think I should—

T: What, no macadamias?!

S: I should fight our great war outside of the White House back at Breitbart.

T: You're gonna fight for me at Breitbart?

S: That's right, whence I shall return.

T: That's a good plan, Steve. Get on the outside. That way everyone thinks we had a big breakup, but the truth is, you're working the heist from the outside. I like it.

S: Yes sir.

T: Here's the point. I got the plan all here. This is an exit interview, but really it's an entry non-interview. You're leaving to do the good work outside. You promise me that you can stay at Breitbart for a while.

S: Yes sir. But when the Wolff book comes out, please don't publicly turn on me.

T: No, of course not, Steve. I would never turn on you publicly. Second, are you going to back the right set of candidates to make me look good?

S: Yes sir. You have my word.

T: Okay. You gonna make sure to wear a green military jacket every time you go to speak at an event?

S: Yes sir.

T: Yeah . . . so you look like that *Romancing the Stone* guy. You look just like Michael Douglas from *Romancing the Stone*.

S: That's what I'm going for.

T: Totally. And that makes me Demi Moore in *Disclosure*! He put his penis in my mouth! He put his penis in my mouth! You remember that movie, Steve?

S: Yes sir.

T: Big virtual reality chase at the end? Reverse sexual discrimination?

S: Yes sir. It was really formative for the way I view the world.

T: Everybody loves *Disclosure*. We should have another screening of it on the White House lawn.

S: Another?

T: Wait. Oooh. Wait a minute.

S: You didn't invite me to a screening of *Disclosure*?

T: Steve—hold on, let me explain this, let me explain. Listen to me. Steve, here's the thing. We were all hanging out—Kellyanne, Steve Miller, you know, the cool crew. And I was like, "Listen. General Kelly's gonna be out of town tonight. What do you say we order Chinese and watch *Disclosure*?" And I gotta tell you, nobody said anything except me. I was like, "Well, Steve's not here, maybe we should wait." And Kellyanne and Steve Miller were like, "No, whatever, it's his loss." And I was like, "Okay, I guess you guys are right." But I felt really bad about it and I want you to know I would have never done it. It was peer pressure! Steve, you're my best friend ever. You're the best guy I ever met!

S: Well, sir, I guess this is goodbye for now.

T: Steve?

S: Yes?

T: Before you go, will you explain the fourth turning to me one more time?

S: Well, sir, there are great ages of human history, and we're at the end of one—

T: Great Asians?

S: Ages. The Hindus believed in it, the Greeks believed in it, and modern mystics believe that—

T: Like Nostradamus?

S: He is not a modern mystic, sir. He was a medieval mystic. He didn't really have much to say about anything. That's a conspiracy theory, I don't buy into that.

T: Like Dionne Warwick?

S: Yes sir.

T: Okay.

S: The fourth turning— We are at the end of an age and at the beginning of a new age and we are uniquely positioned here in the twenty-first century, as celestial events confirm. We have one final opportunity to reconfigure civilization and reinvigorate the power of the great symbols of antiquity. I want American citizenship to be like Roman citizenship. I want to turn our institutions against the elites and return to the absolutism of the classical world.

T: Okay, all right, enough, Steve. Everybody loves Roman. We all know that. Roman Polanski was a great guy. He knew how to get 'em. And get 'em young, you know what I mean. All the directors get 'em young. I should have been a director. Then I could have gotten that Woody tail, you know? That guy got to fuck his daughter! Brigham Young University. When I learned that it wasn't what I thought it was, it was very disappointing. Steve, here's the point. I will make sure to continue the fourth turning for you by buying Celestial Seasons tea. You're going to get fired now from the White House, a book full of things you said is going to come out in six months. You're going to back a bunch of failed Republican candidates and then get fired from everything. Our plan can't fail.

Jack Renegade:
Expulsion

It takes a truly great Great man to rise above the chaos of small unenlightened minds who fail to appreciate the great cycles of the ages which repeat themselves in cosmic time. When great men are corrupted, they cast off those who they once depended on, even their brothers and comrades who made them who they are. The cycles of birth and destruction are as old as that tiny dot of white light that consumed the ether of the pre-universe in the form of an ever-expanding singularity. In other words: An Expulsion.

Jack Renegade pressed the elevator button at the White House, making his final exit from the tomblike corridors of the West Wing. As he walked out of the place, he muttered, "Shithole" to himself.

"What?" said a nineteen-year-old intern boy.

"Nothing. Would you like to come work at Biteblart?"

"No."

"Well, you're losing out, because things are on the upswing for me."

New horizons were around the corner for Jack Renegade. His president had failed him. He had broken all of his promises and betrayed the cause. Jack just couldn't take it anymore. The cobble of the news media and international industrialists had finally gotten a grip on our great leader, neutering his potential like a dog's fat sack. Renegade knew he had lost him. He'd always be there in service if he wanted to turn the ship around, but he knew that wouldn't happen anytime soon. Greener pastures lay ahead for Jack Renegade.

Renegade whistled "Happy Days Are Here Again" as he wandered straight out onto the lawn, past the guard, jumping the gate and getting his sweater and turtleneck caught on the front of it. He dragged it down, ripped the sweater off, and walked away from the White House for what he thought would be the last time.

The only thing Jack regretted leaving behind was the snow globe with his removed cancerous testicle in it. He had promised that he would keep it with him always. But no time for sentimentality: It was time to pick up his weekly check from the Dupratts.

Renegade clicked his heels together and slid clumsily into his 2018 Ferrari Portofino. He revved his engine as he tore down the streets of Washington, tracing the sacred lines of L'Enfant. The president had once said L'Enfant means "the baby" in French. But little did he know this baby had a lot in store for him. Washington was a restless toddler, and the president would soon come to learn that he lost his greatest ally.

Dupratt Mansion, The cold wet stone and sticky iron buzzer reminded all visitors of the brutally majestic legacy of the family whose name it bore. Dozens of beautiful peacocks roamed the grounds. The Dupratts had bred them specifically to have different colors in their feathers to resemble the family crest, and their size and stink were impossible to overstate. Geese were trained to honk on the quarter hour. A really nice fountain. These were truly elegant people. A carriage drawn by four white horses stopped short as Jack crossed its path.

"What are you doing?!" said the carriage man.

"It's me, Jack Renegade."

"Well, you came in the side."

"Oh, really? I come in this way every week. I didn't realize I was entering like a servant."

At that moment, Renegade knew something was wrong, his keen senses were honed in the CIA, MI5, and the NSA after all. He had taken what the Deep State had offered him and cast it aside, knowing one day he would return like Odysseus, transformed and ready to confront the very powers that created him. Was today the day?

He entered the marble hallway, a tribute to Hiram Abiff. Perfect geometry built this place, the sacred messages of the stars and other planes of reality communicating through every single marble step.

His phone beeped: A text from Mr. Dupratt. "Are you here?"

He wrote back: "Yes, I'm in the hallway."

"Where? Which hallway?"

"The sacred one."

"Who let you in?"

"What are you talking about? Who? The horseman."

"We don't have a horseman."

"I don't know."

"Where are you?"

Jack Renegade knew he had to hurry. He tried pushing aside a book on a bookshelf to reveal a secret door, but nothing happened. It seemed he had merely smeared eczema skin on a paperback copy of Paradise Lost. There was no secret door. He started pulling more books off the bookshelf. Dropping more skin. Sweating. Spitting. Stacking big books to make a little seat for himself so he could sit lower and pull more books. Finally, after twenty minutes, Lady Dupratt entered the room.

"What are you doing here? You're ruining the library!"

"Burn them all, I say!"

"No, don't do that. My father wants to speak to you immediately. Didn't he text you? We need to make a change to our arrangement."

The only change Renegade wanted was to stop receiving his weekly payments in worthless fiat currency so he could skip the trip to the Bitcoin machine at CVS in Silver Spring and be paid directly with money backed by the secret primes of Pythagoras which echo the universal harmonics in their mathematical elegance.

Jack sat down with the senior Dupratt, the austere patriarch of the family. Jack saw in his stern face the statuesque ancient lineage of Richard the Third and the Hapsburgs, Rothschilds, and Doolittles. Basically, his eyes were too far apart on a face that was too thin, like a fish. He sat, his royal fingers dancing over the contract. He lifted it gingerly, brushing the parchment once against Jack's wrist. They both let out a gasp. His long, bony fingers were purple from lack of circulation. A pool of water always surrounded his chair. With a swift rip, the contract split in two. His assistant handed Jack a box of his things he had left around the house over the years, along with a check for fifteen dollars. A beer coozie, a Rubik's Cube, an old keychain with keys to a house he no longer owned. His old headphones—there they were. On top of his box of knickknacks was a note in beautiful bold calligraphy that read, "Our relationship is terminated." The bankers or the Deep State must have gotten to him before Jack could have reached him, and now he realized that pool of water was probably piss.

Jack wasn't surprised that a rank sellout like this WASP would betray him like this. As he walked out, he kicked one of the peacocks straight in its big beautiful ass. "I'll set fire to this place!" Renegade shrieked.

He returned hours later with a can of gasoline he filled up at the wholesale club, but he was not allowed through the gate. So he poured it on the front driveway and lit it on fire. Everything was iron, so it just got hot and then cooled down.

Oh my! Jack had almost forgotten he had a date with CNBC's Maria Bartiromo. He and Maria had met on a dating website called Arrow. She had just finished up a hit on Jim Cramer. She was hot and sweaty because Cramer gets crazy on the set. Cramer. Good name. But Jack bought those rights long ago, and that story is for another day.

The coat check girl knew he meant business because he checked four items of clothing and two boxes. Jack Renegade collected himself before sitting down to dinner with television's last leading lady. He ordered his usual: A bottle of bourbon and a hamburger, extra rare, no bun, cold cheese, but the lettuce hot. Jack knew this money honey would give him some advice even if they didn't end up falling in love and living together until the ocean swallowed the world. He told her how things were going. He was too good for the president, but this was all part of a plan as well. He ordered another pound of hamburger meat. Clearly he was being sent on some secret mission of transglobal significance, he explained, but he just didn't know what it was. The people who dispatched him for these types of things hadn't yet told him what this one was about, but it would all come together soon enough he was sure. They were only cutting ties with him because they wanted him to go deep underground.

She looked at him and said, "I don't know what you're talking about. Who do you work for?"

"Try listening next time."

"It sounds to me like you got fired from two jobs today."

He looked at her and winked, but his conjunctivitis made his eye stick for too long. And when he opened it, she was gone.

He'd forgotten to ask her about herself. Time to close out the night by going to his favorite old haunt. The mission would be clear soon enough. One of these people was clearly an agent. Someone had to be telling him what the next move was.

"Excuse me, you need to pay the check."

"What?"

The waiter would have to wait, because it was time for a maneuver called the Dine and Ditch. You make your way to the bathroom and then spend too much time so they think that you're having a problem. Then you get out of there in a mad dash, shoving the coat check clerk and snatching your things.

Jack Renegade walked slowly into Cappy O'Leary's, the hot DC spot where all the congressional aides and Senate advisers drink and gossip. He sat down and ordered himself a gin martini with a shot of bourbon in it. This was his kind of night. He started screaming aloud, "Does anyone have anything for me? Does anyone have anything for me? I work at the White House . . . or I did!"

The bartender presented the drink, but he looked at Jack a little too long, which made Jack wonder: *What's this guy up to? Was he supposed to say something? Was he his secret contact?* Jack gave him a smile. He walked back and served Jack all night. There were no other assets he could find in the bar except this bartender. He watched an entire golf game without talking to anyone. Eventually he realized he was going to close out the place. The bartender looked at Jack again—this time, longer than Jack had ever seen a man look at him before in his life. He knew this must be it. He followed the waiter into the back kitchen. Everyone had left for the night. He said to me, "It'll be two hundred if you want what I think you want."

Jack wasn't used to paying for information, but today was a day full of firsts. He gave the waiter the two hundred, and proceeded to receive the data via a biological delivery system that Jack had never encountered before. The bio-imprinted information exploded into Renegade. Jack waited for the fluid to reach his brain and unpack its secrets.

The next morning, Jack woke up in a bus station with crust butt. He knew he had his mission, though he was still waiting for the nano transference to work its way through his brain to his conscious mind. In the meantime, he had a job to do. Time to get back to work at Biteblart. He stood up and collected his boxes. He heard two passengers getting on the bus say, "Yeah, that's him." Positive ID. His cover had been blown! Renegade had to escape. Jack entered his second trancelike state since dawn. Each vision unlocked the next.

The sun moves in an arc across the sky that the ancients call the great helioplex. The lost knowledge, from Easter Island to the Mayan temples. The great Oroboros snake, its head speaking within the mind of man. It was true, all of these edifices built across time, understanding that the ancients knew a calendar that was greater than we could ever conceive of. Was this the end of a sixty-thousand-year cycle in which the serpent should return to cleanse the earth of the unworthy?

But his SmarTrip Card had expired on the first of the month. The serpent had won yet again. After an unsuccessful hop of the turnstile, he slammed his face into the dirty pavement of the subway floor. Jack Renegade crawled his way into the Metro, narrowly escaping the transit police with a quick whip of the pantaloons. The constables slipped on his slick trousers, and in the rush he left his oily boxers behind as well. Sometimes you have to say goodbye to the past to open up the door to the future.

Biteblart, the top news organization in the United States, was running like a finely tuned machine. People were shuttling paper and pads from desk to desk, writing down the truth as only they could see it and packaging it for an audience eager to be persuaded. Jack said good morning to Marie, the front desk receptionist, who seemed shocked to see him. She shrieked and dropped her papers. She ran into the back, Jack presumed to pre-announce to everyone her joy at his return. The room dropped to silence in an instant. It was so quiet you could hear the humming of the 10-dimensional fibers that create the illusion of existence. From the back of the room he heard a name whispered softly, "Steve?"

Jack turned and barked, "Who's Steve? I'm Jack Renegade."

"Steve," they repeated, "Steve, please come to the office for a second."

Jack would play their game. He agreed and entered. They explained to me that this man they thought Jack was, Steve Bannon, was no longer welcome at Biteblart. They showed a trick mirror in which stood the visage of a bloated, pockmarked clown. This guy was disgusting. That's all Jack could think. Disgusting. Poorly dressed, flaked with psoriasis—a mess. Not the Jack Renegade he knew. Someone dropped a snow globe and the ruffians entered the temple of Solomon and killed Hiram. Three ruffians responsible, representing the three pillars: Doric, Corinthian, and Ionic. The destruction of Joachim and Boaz, we build the universe in our own making.

Archivist's Note

The president wasn't himself lately. Also the two of us hadn't been getting along. Today, corridor rumors had it that he hadn't returned to the residence the night before, so I was extra cautious entering the Oval Office, which was a good thing since opening the side door knocked over a pile of Styrofoam containers that were stacked against the wall. President Trump had the curtains drawn, his hair was flipped to the side, and he had his foot up on the desk. He later told me that he thought he had stubbed his toe because someone had rotated the Oval Office slightly clockwise so things weren't where they were supposed to be. The eyes on the paintings of Washington and Jackson had been blacked out with Sharpie and the red phone was off the hook. A pile of wet magazines sat on one of the couches covering a greasy stain that continued on the carpet. This great man had to retreat from a world that wasn't worthy to be sprayed with his big foamy globs of spit. Shame on them.

But we stand with him. I stand with him. The loyal members of the administration stand with him. And the American people who count stand with him. Because no matter what story the traitors and liars the media and elsewhere are trying to sell, the truth is that Donald J.

Trump is the last hope to prevent this country from falling into the abyss. Peg hadn't returned my calls. I hadn't returned the divorce papers. So we were in a standoff, maybe the same one we'd been in for twenty-five years before I woke up. She was a snake. Like Cohen, like Flynn, like all the cowards who had betrayed my king. I repeated what the president was muttering into his morning McGriddle: "They're all going to pay."

LAWYERS, SONS, AND MONEY

CALL: MICHAEL COHEN VOICE MAIL (11/4/2013)

Voice mail: Hey, this is Michael Cohen. I got a new phone, so leave your name and number and I'll give you a call when I get back. Bad-abing!

Trump: Michael! Hello? Hello? Michael, are you there? He's not picking up. Michael, this is Trump. Listen, I think the meeting went really great in Russia. Russia, the Miss Universe. I think we got the permits, we just need the bank guy and the permit guy to get together with us. And I got that letter of intent and I intend to do it! We're gonna sign the deal and it's gonna be so big. And I know you were talking to me about all these guys who can put money through the apartments and I figured out what we can do. We'll have three apartments furnished that we can resell over and over again and then we just hire some people to be in the apartment if anyone goes to check it out. And then we have, like, a family there, they're the extended family of whoever, the Russian oil guy. Grandpa, Grandma, couple of cousins, that should be good. Unky, Auntie, a couple of babies, a little nephew, Grandpappy. We'll have 'em all, and they'll all live in there, and we can shift them around, we can pay them—you know, in Russia you can pay them nothing, okay? And then, I was also thinking, I know that Putin's guy was talking about a place to keep women, and I think that the fourth through the seventh floors would be perfect places for girls to turn tricks, do whatever you want to do. It's an easy access, you don't need a hotel key to get into the building, so it's easy for guys to get up there. And I say we make a website, and do the whole thing. And I'm hoping when we go over there for this next Miss Universe visit we can, uh, sample the product. I know Melania doesn't know I'm going, I'm not gonna tell her till I'm at the airport, so this should be a good time for us. We're gonna have some fun, Cohen, just you and me! You know, you get that dick wet finally, you know. Get that dick wet, you know? Get your pecker wet. Get your pecker wet, Michael. Bye, I love you!

CALLS: BLOCKED NUMBER TO DONALD TRUMP JR.
(6/9/2016)

3:10 p.m.

Trump: I can't believe it. Oh my god. We're such sneaks. We're such sneakies, Donnie.

D: Dad, stay upstairs.

T: I'm gonna stay up—oh my god, oh my god, though! I so wanna come down, I so wanna come downstairs.

D: I want you here, but they say we gotta keep you separate. Paul, Felix, Jeff. Papadopoulos. Everybody says you stay upstairs. Go to your office, go to your apartment. They're gonna have some good stuff for us, Dad. Don't worry, I'll tell you as soon as I know anything.

T: It's so sneaky, though. It's so sneaky, Don Jr.! It's like, you're only three floors below me, I'm right upstairs and I know everything! But I don't know anything, you know what I mean? Don't worry, I don't know anything.

D: Exactly.

T: Because you're talking about the babies—everybody loves the babies, and who wouldn't want us to figure out how to get more babies into the America?

D: We're talking about the voting machines, though.

T: I know that, you idiot! Listen to me. We've got it all covered. The babies is the cover story and it's gonna work. But I want to hear they're hacking the voting booths or, like, what they're doing with that Cambridge Anal Fistula. Doing whatever business they're doing. Whatever they're gonna do. Cambridge Anal Fistula is doing all the good science, but we need to know what's the dirt I wanna know on Hillary, okay? Is she doing the pizza kids? What's happening, okay? So you're gonna call me, okay? You're gonna call me. And when you call me, I'm gonna call you. I'm gonna call you. When I call you, okay? It's gonna be from a blocked number, okay? But we'll say it's the babies.

D: Oh, that's smart, Dad. But how will I know it's you?

T: What?

D: How will I know it's you?

T: Because I'm the only blocked number calling you, you idiot?

D: But how will I know you're calling if I can't see it?

T: Because it says "Blocked Number," you moron. And here's the fool-proof part: You can't *69. You can't *69 a blocked number. So there's no callbacks. Nobody can call it back. And everyone is saying blocked numbers are totally untraceable. So there's like no way, you know what I mean? So it's like, we used to do it all the time when we'd prank Chinese food restaurants, and we'd do a merged call, so we'd put one Chinese food restaurant on with another one, and then they'd be talking to one another and they'd both be saying, "Who called who?!"

D: And their names were Hu?

T: No. They're just saying, "Who called who." Like who—

D: Because one of their names was Hu.

T: No! None of their names were Who. I don't know what their names are, you idiot. I'm saying who like Who, like an owl. Who.

D: All right, they're here, so. They're waiting for me, so—

T: Ooh! Ooh! Ooh! Good good good good. Okay okay, go in there and then call me. No, I'll call you!

3:28 p.m.

D: Hello?

T: Hello! Stranger calling from a blocked number!

D: Uh, who is this?

T: Oh, are you an idiot? It's me, your father.

D: Oh, hey Dad. I was just—

T: Don't call me Dad, it's a blocked number!

D: Okay. Uh, I was just—they were talking about how they can get emails if we say when the sanctions will go away, so, I don't know, seems like a real possibility.

T: Okay, so. If we do this, if we promise to make the sanctions go away, then you're saying they can do the thing with the election, yeah?

D: Well, they said first it's Hillary dirt, then second it's voting day stuff that they didn't want to say.

T: Voting day stuff? You're my eyes and my ears, you idiot. Why aren't you paying attention in there? I mean, my god! I don't even understand what you're talking about!

D: I mean, the woman wasn't even hot. She was just a lawyer.

T: Listen to me. You're not in there—this isn't like that time I took you to that cathouse to lose your virginity. It doesn't matter about the lawyer.

D: Well, my wife—things aren't going too well.

T: Yeah, I know, okay? And I got a beautiful girl I'm going to hook you up with. All right? But if you want Daddy to give you the girl, then you gotta give me the election.

D: Okay, Dad, I'm going back in.

T: Go in there—tell them—listen to me! Hello?!

3:44 p.m.

T: Who's this?

D: Dad, I tried to call your blocked number but it didn't work so I blocked mine to call you.

T: No, you can't call back to the blocked number, I gotta call you, you moron! This is my office line!

D: Sessions said it didn't matter because they can tell anyway, even a blocked number doesn't help.

T: No, that's not true. Everyone knows a blocked number can't be traced.

D: Well, Flynn says the FBI has got a better *69.

T: No, there's no better *69. What would the star-number even be?

D: Seventy?

T: Shut up and tell me what they said.

D: There's, uh, they said that they can get Hillary emails, they said that they're in most of the voting systems in different states in the country, and they said that we can build the tower in Moscow. All we gotta do is drop the sanctions and change the rules about the Ukraine, throw some tariffs on some metals, and something else, I wrote it down.

T: Listen to me. Tell them we'll drop the sanctions, of course we'll arm the Ukraine—what do I care? Do the Ukraine. Do the Ukraine.

D: Why don't you call me back from your blocked number and I'll conference you in.

T: Okay. Hold on. But it's gotta stay silent, okay? It's gotta stay silent. Nobody can know. All right, go back in the meeting.

D: Okay. Call me back from the blocked number and I'll merge you in on the call we're already on right now.

T: Okay, got it!

3:46 p.m.

Unidentified Russian: So it is most important for our interests that—

T: Hello?

R: No—is this Donald Trump?

T: Yeah, it's me.

Papadopolis: Sir, you really shouldn't be—we shouldn't have you in this meeting, sir.

T: Don't worry, my number is blocked. Nobody knows I'm here. Just call me David.

P: All right, sir, the meeting is just wrapping up.

T: No, wait—talk—

Jeff Sessions: Don Jr. just kept stepping out into the hallway because his phone kept ringing.

T: Right. Don't worry about it, that was nobody. Listen, we have to talk for at least twenty seconds about something else until the feds stop listening, okay?

R: The feds—if they're listening, the meeting is over. We talk adoption.

T: No no no! Let's talk about uh, uh, let's talk about the dishes. Boy, those dishes are real clean, did you finish washing them?

R: Who are you talking to?

T: I'm talking to you. You're my Russian housekeeper.

R: No. I am an attorney.

D: Dad, they're packing up.

JS: Uh, I'm—I'm the housekeeper, me, uh, Jeff Sessions. I'm the housekeeper, oh sir, I washed those plates up real good, sir!

T: Those are good plates, good job, Jeff, and look at your apron! It's got a beautiful chicken on it!

JS: Oh, child. Oh child, you are the living end, child. Now let me fry you up some catfish there, sugar.

T: There we go. Very good. And by the way, Jeff, I'd like you to act like that all the time from now on.

JS: Oh save me Lord!

CALL: MICHAEL COHEN VOICE MAIL (9/24/2016)

VM: Hi, you've reached Michael Cohen. I can't get to the phone right now, so leave me a message, *capisce?*

Trump: Hello? Hello? Michael? Voice mail. Michael, this is Trump. Listen, I think we're gonna win this thing. It's looking real good. You see that thing? You see Hillary? You see Hillary the other day, shaking around getting into that van? Oh man. Pretty funny stuff. I gotta give it to her, she's a tough lady. That's a tough lady to stick it out. Very tough. It's gonna be tough in the next debate. Anyway, listen. Things are going so great, and it looks like we have a chance. Now, who knows. At the end of the day, we can't predict anything. But I want to make sure we have all our ducks in a row. You know? Get the ducks, line 'em up. When you see that mother duck walking those babies across the street, they're all in a row. And you gotta make way for ducklings! You gotta make way. They have a street sign with the duck on it. Hard to find. And can the ducks read the sign? I don't get it. Ducks can tell the sign, they know where to cross? I don't think so. Anyway, we need to make sure that we take care of the Russia thing. Very important that you get the thing and I want you to talk to the guy. The one who had the cheeks like they were apricot pits? They were all rotty? Like that guy from all the movies in the '80's. You know, he had a real acne thing! We're gonna build that tower, Michael! We're gonna get in Russia, I can feel it. But

I need to know, I need to know that it's all right and that everything's done and that you put all the documents and that anything—especially the meeting in Russia is very important. Now, we went over Miss Universe. I want the flight logs buried, okay? I don't want anyone to know I was there. And also you gotta take care of that girl. Make sure all the girls are paid off before we get into the next stage of this thing, okay? A hundred g's should do it, plus a little for you—I mean, these girls have never seen that kind of money in their life. So that should be good. Uhh—by the way, going to Mar-a-Lago this weekend, love for you to come down. We're going to get some good honeys there, some choice honeys, so bring some extra money because we're going to have to pay them off, if you know what I mean. You know what I mean? I love you, I'll talk to you later. Bye bye!

CALL: MICHAEL COHEN VOICE MAIL (3/1/2017)

VM: Hi, you've reached Michael Cohen on my brand-new cell phone! Please leave a message and I'll call you back. Bye bye!

Trump: Michael? Michael? Hello? Listen, uh, did you move that money to that guy? The guy? The Shatner guy, Shtayner, whatever his name is? I gotta tell you, I'm confused. Because this medallion guy, I thought it was William Shatner. And I'm looking at the spelling, and it's not that. So I'm a little disappointed because I thought we were giving $26 million to William Shatner. And, I was so excited because he was the best captain. It's too bad he died in the Nexus. He's trapped there for all of eternity, just like Captain Picard's trapped in British Christmas! But I don't think that's too bad, I'd love to be trapped in British Christmas for the rest of my life. So I want you to move another $16 million over to this guy, okay? And make sure that it's untraceable. Because these medallions, they're dropping in price. Have you seen it? The Uber's ruining it! It went from a million to two hundred thousand. It's a crazy depreciation. Shatner probably does need the money. He lost his son on the Genesis Planet, which was very sad. And it was a Priceline deal, which made it even worse. Oh, also, listen. There's this—Stormy. Remember the Stormy girl? Um, she's starting to talk to people. I'm hearing word that she's talking to people. And I don't like it, I think it's very terrible, it's a terrible thing. And you know, these are all lies, Michael. These are lies. And we know that they're lies. And we need to make sure that she understands that she can't be telling untruths she's saying that are true. So I need you to find a guy, get a good guy, big guy, just approach her in Vegas, okay, just let her know where everything stands. Make sure you get a guy that a sketch artist would not be able to draw, someone who's got, I dunno, too general of a face or something like that, someone too hard for a sketch artist to do. And here's what I think he should say, he should say, "You want your mommy to get beat up?" And he says it to the baby. And he goes, "Coochie coochie," at the end. And that's gonna scare the baby. And the baby's gonna go, "Mommy, Mommy, don't do this. Be good to Trump." The baby's gonna know. Cause the babies all love me. If babies could have voted for me I would have won by a lot more. But babies can't vote and we need to change that. Babies on the voter rolls for 2020. Make sure all babies, even preemies. Anyway, listen, also, I'm getting a little nervous about the FBI and the people—so you should probably start getting rid of that old box you have with all the old phones in it. Start getting rid of all the old phones from the box. I really suggest doing it this week. Burn the papers, put things away, lock them away in undisclosed areas. I don't know, Michael, I'm getting very nervous. And listen, get to the cloud. Whatever you do, Michael, get to the cloud!

CALL: MIKE FLYNN, FORMER NATIONAL SECURITY ADVISOR (4/25/2017)

Flynn: Hello?

Trump: Flynn. It's me.

F: Mr. President?

T: Okay, don't say the name. It's me.

F: You shouldn't be calling me here, sir.

T: Just call me . . . Bennigan's . . . Restaurant.

F: What?

T: That's my code name! Call me Bennigan's Restaurant. Okay? How you holding up?

F: I'm fine, sir, but we really shouldn't be talking. I can't say more than that.

T: Listen, you gotta stay strong, you understand me?

F: Yes sir.

T: You gotta stay strong.

F: I'll do my best, sir.

T: I don't care what they do to you, you remember that you have friends on the inside. I got a lot of people who've had to do time, who've had to go in the birdcage. And I don't mean the gay one with Robin Williams.

F: Yes sir.

T: So what've they been asking you?

F: I really can't say, sir. Sir, I'm answering the questions they ask me as honestly as I can.

T: Why? You're supposed to dodge, clam up. I mean, you're gonna— listen—

F: Please don't tell me that. Please don't say that.

T: If you go away, you're going to a nice, beautiful prison suite. They're gonna slice the garlic so thin it's gonna melt in the pan, okay?

F: Sir, I don't think you can promise me that, and I don't think you should promise me anything. I'm not planning on going to prison, sir. But we shouldn't be talking.

T: Why, because the phones are tapped? We know they tap. They love to tap. But now that we know they tap, why would they keep listening? Because we wouldn't say anything.

F: Exactly.

T: Why would we say anything since we know they're on?

F: Exactly.

T: Exactly. So what about the thing about the thing?

F: I don't know which thing, sir.

T: The guy, the thing with the guy.

F: I think they might know about all that, sir.

T: All of it?!

F: I think so, sir.

T: Even the thing with the guy who picked up the thing? And put the thing back down?

F: Are you talking about the lunch order?

T: It's all about the lunch. You can't tell them about it. Listen, first off, you can't let anyone know I had Wendy's, because it was a code burger, okay? It's a square. The secret shape.

F: Yes sir.

T: Second, I've known a lot of guys who've gone up the river. Johnny, Little Tips, Mr. Hats, Low Down Dickie, Martin, Rowan, Boat Boy, Sipplesix, The Skunk, Debby the Cake Queen, Roger Roger, Ricky Scaggs.

F: Yes sir. I understand, sir.

T: Roy Orbison.

F: I think he died, sir.

T: Tom Petty. George Harrison. Oh, wait a minute, I'm reading off my CD shelf.

F: Yes sir.

T: Listen to me, Flynn. You wanna see your son alive again?

F: Sir, please, let's not go down this road.

T: What did you tell him. What did you tell Mueller?!

F: Sir, I have to get off the phone.

T: Tell Mueller! You betrayed me! Did you betray me?! Did you talk trash? Did you tell them about everything? Did you tell them about my little dance breaks? You tell them how I put my pinky up when I have a coffee?

F: No sir, no sir.

T: You tell them our inside joke about my frequent bathroom breaks?

F: Please sir, don't make me say.

T: You tell them about that my whole company is propped up by foreign crime syndicate cash? That Trump Tower is just one big money-laundering operation full of empty apartments bought at above-market rates by Russian oligarchs and that since I've been president our foreign policy is being sold off to the highest bidder through shell companies owned by my mob lawyer? Did you tell him that?

F: Yes sir.

T: Ohhh, no!

CALL: MICHAEL COHEN (2/1/2018)

Trump: Michael. What's going on up there, Michael?

Michael Cohen: Don't worry, sir. It's under control.

T: Michael, I don't like this!

M: It's under control, sir.

T: Michael, this is not good.

M: We gotta handle on everything, sir. The NDA is airtight, the money got paid out, she's digging her own grave, so to speak.

T: I mean, this bitch—this is unbelievable. This is unbelievable. She signed the paperwork! She said she would do it. And now she's going back on her word.

M: She took the money, sir, I know.

T: She's a total Indian giver. Total Indian giver.

M: Don't worry, sir, you just stay above the fray. Stay out of it, sir. You stay out of it, sir, you stay out of it, as far as you're concerned I gave her a gift.

T: Why would you give her a gift? That's the dumbest cover story ever.

M: Because that's it, that's the story. I gave her the gift.

T: What a stupid story, Michael. What are you, crazy? No one's gonna believe that.

M: It's gonna work fine, sir, you just stay out of it.

T: I don't know. Why would you give her a gift?

M: Because. I'm a generous guy.

T: I don't buy it. I'm sorry.

M: I understand, sir, but just stay out of it. Do you understand?

T: I mean, can you believe what she's saying? That—I mean—first off, listen. You and I both know the thing that we don't know that we know is true, okay? And we know it's true. And I'm gonna say something else. She says I was sitting on the end of the bed? I was sitting on the end of the bed like a little boy? Are you kidding me? I was not sitting—I was standing up, I was rock hard, standing there waiting for her. She tried to spank me with that magazine and I caught it and I looked at her right in the eye and said, "I think we need to go up to my room." And she said yeah! And she was the one who took the magazine, not me. And you know what? You know what nobody knows? I made a little fart when she hit me with the magazine. I got the last word on that. You can get the DNA off that magazine, you'll see. A little poop puff. That'll be the—the little poop marks the time line! Do that. Call forensics in. Get the DNA!

M: Sir, sir—Donald, listen to me. Don't overthink it.

T: Mr. President.

M: Trump—

T: Mr. President.

M: Listen to me. You stay out of it. This happened a long time ago, we took care of it. You don't have to worry about it.

T: Oh, Michael, you shut up. You shut up, you dweeb-faced, sunken-eyed garbage heap.

M: All right, sir.

T: You sit in your stupid office or your dumb hotel room and you make up lies, and I know what you do, you screw everything up. That's what you do. You haven't done anything right in your whole goddamn life!

M: All right, sir, just—

T: You don't have a single thing to show for your whole goddamn life.

M: This conversation's over.

T: Your wife should be ashamed of you—

M: You stay quiet and forget this conversation happened—

T: Your wife and your stupid children. Your dumb ugly children. I haven't spent any time with you and your dumb ugly children. I'll ruin you. You think I'll save you? I'll take you apart. You do anything I'll take you apart, you get me? You know. You know? We buried that body so many years ago and you're gonna bring that up to me now? You're gonna bring that up to me now?!

M: She's the one who came forward, sir, and I'm handling it.

T: You're not handling anything. You couldn't even handle your two-inch pudd. I knew I shouldn't have ever gotten a Jewish lawyer. Okay, now what about the McDougal, there's more than one.

M: There's several, sir.

T: There's so many, Michael, there's so many!

M: Don't worry, sir, the agreements are airtight, sir. You have nothing to worry about.

T: But the McDougal—that was paid off by somebody else, we can't control that.

M: Well, it's all third-party, sir. We really don't have control over it at this point other than what the agreement says. And the agreement says that they can't talk, so if they talk, they owe us a lot of money.

T: Uhh, they owe us a lot of money?

M: Yes, sir. They have to pay back the money.

T: Well, then tell them all to talk! This is perfect, Michael. I mean, we need to get money. We need to make more money.

M: No sir.

T: What we could do is— Wait a minute, I got a perfect idea. Get all of them to flip. Make sure they all start talking. Make 'em all breach their NDAs.

M: Sir, I don't think you're thinking about the—

T: I'm thinking of money, Michael! We could make like a hundred, two hundred million dollars off this!

M: I don't think you're thinking through the ramifications of this, sir. I think you should—

T: Ramifications. That's a choice word. God knows every one of those girls had a ramification.

M: Most of them would disagree, sir.

T: You know I can't believe her. I can't believe what she said. And what, what, she didn't enjoy it? Seemed like she was enjoying it when her face was turned away from me and she was making no sound.

M: She's a porn actress, sir, so if she wasn't able to fake it for you, I don't know what to tell you.

T: What the hell are you talking about. She wasn't faking it. Don't you understand? It's the inverse with porn stars. If you have sex with a porn star and they totally shut down and lay there like a stone-dead body with their face still and completely silent, that for them is relaxing! Because most of the time they have to perform and go, "Ooh, ooh, oh oh, ooh ooh, oh, that cock, that cock, ooh ooh oh, my pussy my pussy!" But there—

M: Where are you right now, sir?

T: Where? I'm in a cabinet meeting! The press is here! Yeah, I'll take questions in a second! Anyway, okay? Listen. Who do we have. We have Stormy Daniels. The storm surge. And the waves are flowing everywhere.

M: Her real name is Stephanie Cliffords, sir. That's important to remember.

T: Clifford? The big red dog? Double it!

INTERVIEW: CALM BEFORE THE STORMY

Trump: Things aren't looking too good, Kelsey.

Kelsey Nelson: I wouldn't be too worried, sir. It's in your nature to seduce women. You can't be constrained. No one expects you to behave the way normal men have to.

T: You know it. Write that down. You know the kind of guy I am. They can't keep their hands off me, you know. They can't keep their hands off me. They love a piece of Trump. They love a piece of Trump. And I can't stop myself. But I'll tell you this. She is a liar. I mean, a total liar. We had a great time. And I have the tapes to prove it.

K: You have a tape, sir?

T: I have all the tapes. I recorded—I called her and I recorded all the phone calls. Just like a jerky boy. Like a total jerky boy. Frank Rizzo! Who was a Democrat. But I want you to hear them and you tell me what. I think we should release them.

K: Are you sure you want this on the record, sir?

T: Yeah it's all on the record!

Trump presses play on a 1980s Sony Dictaphone tape recorder with the little tapes.

Trump: Hello, Stormy, hello?

Stormy: Oh, Donald.

T: You don't sound happy, is there another Donald you don't like so much?

S: No.

T: I gotta tell you, I'm missing you. I'm missing you so much. God, that was so good. That was so good. You remember? You remember how we were really flirting, huh? We were really flirting.

S: Yeah . . . so I wanted to talk to you about the show, *The Apprentice*—

T: Oh, yeah, we're gonna do it, we're gonna do it, it's gonna be incredible.

S: Well, I might hold you to that.

T: Yeah, yeah, you can hold me. Hold all of it.

S: If you're serious about me interviewing about the show, we could have another—

T: Hold all of it. You know what I mean? You know what I mean when I say, "Hold all of it"?

S: All right.

T: You can hold it all.

S: Maybe we'll have a meeting in public.

T: I mean, you're a professional. You can hold it all.

S: Look, I had a fine time with you. We had a good night. A good time.

T: It was a tremendous time. And the love, the love. There was such love there. And nobody spoke to me—I never let anyone speak to me the way you spoke to me.

S: Well, that's cute—

T: You're a tough gal.

S: That's very sweet.

T: Strong woman. I love it.

S: That's very sweet.

T: Not like my wife.

S: How is your wife?

T: Oh, you know, uh, the baby, is, uh, four months or something, I don't know. She's good, whatever, you know, it's really not working with us, it's not working with us—

S: I'm sorry to hear that.

T: And she said, you know, she said to me, she said, "Listen, Donald, you need to do what you gotta do, you need to do, I have the baby, I have the baby," and you know how it works. Down there is not working, you know, cause they had to cut her. They had to cut her to get the baby out.

S: You know, I really wanted to talk about some business—

T: And—

S: I wanted to talk about the television show—

T: And she said to me, "We have an open marriage, we have an open marriage, and it's fine. Donald, do whatever you want."

S: I know, you told me this.

T: But I just don't want—Stormy—

S: You told me this the other night.

T: Excuse me—

S: You told me this the other night and that's all fine.

T: But you can't say anything, that's the only thing.

S: I wasn't planning to.

T: You see, because she doesn't want to be embarrassed. She's fine with it but she doesn't want to know about it and no one else can know about it, right?

S: I understand. I really mainly just wanted to talk about *The Apprentice,* you know, I'm making my schedule for the year, and I—

T: You making that schedule with your tits? You making that schedule with your wet tits? Am I making you hot? Am I making you hot?

S: It's ten in the morning and my daughter—I have to take my daughter—

T: Ooh, yeah your daughter.

S: —to swim class. Oh, please don't—

T: Ooh, swimming.

S: Please stop that now. I'll ignore that because I know you just react to what you think you might hear—

T: How old's your daughter?

S: She's two years old.

T: Oh, ohh, uhh—Ohh, uhhh, ohhh—hello?

S: I'm still here.

T: I thought you said twenty-two. Because then we could have some fun, you know? Some mother/daughter, mother/daughter fun. You know? Mummy and daughter teaching each other the ropes? Learning where their sensitive parts are? Being guided by me?

S: So, is there a possibility with a meeting with NBC or is this going to be what we talk about?

T: Oh, yeah, all of them.

S: And the production company—

T: NBC, ABC, CBS—

S: Is there someone I can talk to about getting that on the books? And it would be NBC? Because that's the network that airs your show.

T: HBO . . . Cinemax. Well we're gonna meet with them all. Stormy, you're a real talent. And I want to make sure that you meet with them all. And I got a guy, he's gonna set up all the meetings. As soon as I can get in touch with him. We're gonna fly you down to New York, you're gonna be on the show. I think it's a great idea. This porn star turned businesswoman. It's a great idea. And there's a lot of work for you in it, honey. There's a lot of work for you. What are you doing in a couple hours? We could meet about it.

S: I'm going to be at swim class with my daughter—

T: Ooh, yeah.

S: My two-year-old daughter.

T: Oh, what?! Oh . . . Uh, oh! Oh god, what am I doing. What am I doing? Get out of here! Melania, I'm on the phone!

K: That's all?

Trump: Click! So, there's nothing to worry about. I think I come off looking like a peach!

Trump: So, a week goes by, Kelsey, and she won't stop! It's like a total extortion.

Kelsey: I don't want to listen to another conversation, sir.

T: So then I recorded this conversation.

(click)

T: Hi, I'm recording. Hello?
Stormy: Hello.

T: Hello?

S: Hello, Donald.

T: Ooh, hi.

S: Donald, could you call my agent, he says that nobody at NBC has heard anything about our deal.

T: Ahh. I get hard hearing your voice!

S: I really want to get the ball rolling—Donald, if this isn't going to be real, that's okay. We had a nice night, it was good to get to know you. If there's gonna be no movement on the show—

T: Oh, I had a movement. I had a big one this morning. I would have been so ready. All emptied out. If you had come over, like I asked you to, I would have been totally hollow. Today's the first time I've never had any doody in my body. And that's when the best sex happens.

S: Donald, you're a good guy.

T: I know. Let's go out. Dinner.

S: Maybe.

T: And kisses?

S: I don't want to just go to your hotel room. Maybe we go out, we meet about the show, about work.

T: I have an idea. What if we come to my hotel room, have dinner there. We can FaceTime one of my friends. And then we get to business.

S: All right. That's not—that's not fun for me. Do you understand that? Do you understand that that's not a lot of fun for me?

T: The dinner? I get it, let's cut the dinner and skip to the fun part.

S: I don't want to come to your hotel room and have sex for ten minutes and then go home.

T: Ten minutes?! Yeah, you're right. Uh, you wanna meet somewhere else?

S: Listen, if you weren't serious about—

T: Like a public park or something? Kinky, kinky.

S: I still want to talk about *The Apprentice*, because the entire reason I met with you the first time was that you told me that maybe you'd want to have me on *The Apprentice* and you're stringing me along like I'm—

T: The guy never called?

S: No, nobody's called me or my agent.

T: John Barron never called?

S: John Barron didn't call.

T: He's here right now. Hold on, I'll put him on the phone.

S: Wait a second, you said you were in—

T: Hello, it's John Barron.

S: Donald.

T: Hello, John Barron.

S: Donald.

T: This is John Barron! I'm the publicist.

S: What is this?

T: Listen, I'm working real hard trying to get you on *The Apprentice*. It's just, we're hitting a couple of snafus. You know, the best idea would probably be to meet with Mr. Trump in his hotel room later tonight.

S: I'm not doing that.

T: Yeah, uh, okay, well, what are you wearing right now? It's important because I need to give a profile to NBC.

S: I'm wearing my equestrian uniform. I'm wearing breeches.

T: Ooh, breeches.

S: And a jacket.

T: Oh, whoa.

S: A hat.

T: Oh, yeah.

S: I'm at the stable. I'm about to ride a horse.

T: I'm a horse. I'm John Barron. I'm a stallion, I'm a horse.

S: Can you put Donald back on?

T: I got a big old horse cock.

S: Because even Donald wasn't quite this bold with me on the phone, and it's the middle of the day.

T: No, but John Barron's bold. John Barron would do anything. John Barron's uhh, uhh, you wanna horse between your legs? Hello? Hello? Hold on, I'll put Trump on.

S: Donald, please.

T: It's me. Boy that John Barron's a real pig.

S: Why's he in your bedroom at nine in the morning?

T: Cause we're going over publicity! Here's the point. NBC says it's gonna be tough. And that I need to have a few more meetings with you so I can really figure out what's the special thing about you and we can't do that over the phone. We need to do it in person, and preferably in a hotel room because that's where I'm most comfortable. So, it's—listen. I want you on there. Everyone wants you on there. NBC's so close, they're so close. But there's a lot of opportunity. A lot of great work opportunity. But it requires you to get along, to play along.

S: I'm not—I don't think I'm going to do this anymore. It was nice meeting you, and we had a night, and I think that's going to be the end of it for me.

T: Oh, whoa. Really? Oh, so you don't like me? You don't like me?

S: I like you fine—

T: Oh, so you just use me? You use me to get on this TV show and you don't like me? You don't like who I am? Oh, I'm sorry. Who is it, some big tough boring guy, is that who you're into? Some guy with his big cock and his big abs, that's what you're into? A black guy like your friend is into?

S: I'm not having this conversation.

T: You're not into personality? You're not into someone with a great personality who also knows how to make love? Glamour? Glitz? Class? The lights? All the limos? Oh, I'm sorry you can't handle it, Stormy. I'm sorry. I'm sorry that I gave you my love and I gave you my heart and all you did was use me. So you used me. So you're just basically a whore. You're just basically a whore, that's all you are.

(click)
(to Kelsey)

T: So you heard it all now. Don't you think everyone owes Trump an apology?

SARS SPREADING THE NEWS

SUSPICIOUS ACTIVITY REPORT

FROM: TELLER #7719 HOLLIS, NY

Customer C█████████ opened three new accounts today, making cash deposits of $250,000 into each. Customer kept making small talk with me throughout the transaction, commenting frequently on the stuffed frog I have at my teller desk. "That's a great frog, really green." He repeated the compliment a few times. He added customer name Olaf ▓▓▓▓▓▓▓ as a joint owner of all three accounts. Business Account #▓▓▓▓▓▓▓ was assigned to business entity "Essential Consultants LLC," Account #▓▓▓▓▓▓ to business entity "Necessary Advisers," and Account #▓▓▓▓▓▓▓ to be entity "Indispensable Specialists, Inc." Customer was sweating a lot and muttering about my decorative frog as well as reading the FDIC sticker fine print to himself during the transaction. When Customer C▓▓▓▓▓▓ left I noticed my frog was gone.

SUSPICIOUS ACTIVITY REPORT

FROM: AML SUPERVISOR, FARMINGDALE, NY

Customer Cohen triggered automatic alert to AML dept after wire transfers totaling $2.25 million were sent to 3 accounts in $750,000 increments (#▓▓▓▓▓▓, #▓▓▓▓▓▓, #▓▓▓▓▓▓). AML specialist reports that Cohen answered a phone call to the number on file and reassured specialist that the funds was domestically sourced. When confronted with AML dept. conclusion that funds were sent through ▓▓▓▓▓▓ third-party money-transfer service provided by ▓▓▓▓▓▓ Iranian financial institution (an OFAC blocked country) customer C▓▓▓▓▓▓ became irate and asked specialist "what [his] fucking problem was." Supervisor attempted to speak to Mr. Cohen earlier today leaving a voice mail with beeper messaging service. Supervisor received return call from unknown third party identifying himself as Dennis ▓▓▓▓▓▓. Transcription unavailable as caller was whispering and unintelligible. Supervisor recalls that caller insisted that there must be some confusion and that the money was sourced from a Korean food service company ██████████. Upon contacting ████████████ and inquiring about this information, Supervisor learned that ████████████ is a private military contracting service operating out of the DPRK. In a subsequent call, Cohen representative Dennis ████ ██ ████" Please Advise.

SUSPICIOUS ACTIVITY REPORT

FROM TELLER #7719, HOLLIS, NY

Olaf ████████████ attempted to withdraw $500,050 dollars today. Very polite and even flirtatious, I'm not saying anything, but he was fine! He complemented my new desk frog. Unfortunately, moments after his withdrawal, he was discovered a block away from the bank with a puncture in the back of his skull. Linda found him while walking to Chipotle. Flagging all three accounts.

SUSPICIOUS ACTIVITY REPORT

FROM: TELLER #7719, HOLLIS, NY

Customer C████████████ has requested that $300,000 dollars be transferred to a Rhona ████████████ aka Titty Caca aka Miss Milky Craps. He also brought a stuffed turtle and presented it to me. He said, "Your frog could use a friend; everyone needs friends. Friends stick together. Could you imagine if this turtle told everyone about the frog's personal business, it might be the end of BOTH of them." He placed a Polaroid photo on my desk, and asked me to do what I could to keep his transaction private and unlogged. When he left I turned it over. The picture showed my original desk frog in a dank basement rubber banded to a little chair with lit matches jammed in his eyes. Please Advise.

SUSPICIOUS ACTIVITY REPORT

FROM: AML SUPERVISOR, FARMINGDALE, NY

Transfer request from ▮▮▮▮▮▮▮▮ based in UAE in the amount of $1.25 million from C▮▮▮▮▮▮ Account #▮▮▮▮▮▮▮. Unable to verify business address, I contacted Customer C▮▮▮▮▮▮. I could hear a conversation in the background. His self-identified business partner Dennis ▮▮▮▮▮▮ took the phone and asked me how much money I made and if I knew who he was. Customer Cohen returned to the call saying that the money was a private investment in a tech company, "Zorin Industries," he was considering doing business with. No record of this company exists, but a Google search provided a reference to it in the 1985 James Bond film *A View to a Kill.*" I asked if he was referring to a fictional company in a spy movie. Before customer C▮▮▮▮▮▮ could answer, he was interrupted again by his associate Dennis ▮▮▮ ▮▮▮▮▮▮. He said "▮▮▮▮▮▮, hello, haven't you heard of it? The CEO is an albino! He flies high atop the clouds in an incredible blimp!" Transcript indicates that a fourth party in the background referred to associate as "Mr. President." Looking to verify call number and amount.

CALL: ESSENTIAL CONSULTANTS (1/18/2018)

Felicity Financial: Hello?

Essential Consultants: Hi, you've reached Essential Consultants. If you are calling about insights into the president's thinking, press 1. If you are calling because you are an adult movie actress or model who needs to keep her mouth shut, press 2. For all other calls, press 0.

(beep)

EC: Hello, Essential Consultants?

F: Hi, this is Dave Brock from Felicity Financial. I'm looking into a recent transfer to account 00988824 in the amount of $775,000.

EC: Yes, I mean, we have any number of accounts. We appreciate your business.

F: Well, this is specifically the account number I just gave you.

EC: Well, we have many.

F: I understand that, you have many but that's irrelevant. I wanted to know specifically about this account and the money transferred into it. Felicity usually flags anything over $250,000 for large transactions to third-world nations and we noticed that this was going to Niger. And we're concerned obviously about security and fraudulent transfer of funds.

EC: Okay, well, um, thank you very much, but we're not interested, and we'd like to be removed from your list, please.

F: I'm not a telemarketer. I'm the vice president of AML at Felicity and I'm very concerned about this money transfer. So again, if I could get the information on that account number and what the transfer routing was, it would really help my day.

EC: Okay, well, I guess, uh, I'll have to talk to my supervisor. Can I talk to your supervisor?

F: The president of the bank is my supervisor, technically, but he's—

EC: And is he available? Because if I put my supervisor on he's going to want to talk to *your* supervisor.

F: She is obviously very very busy with a number of different responsibilities—

EC: So is my supervisor—

F: Again, I don't think there's a relative relationship, which is that I probably would be above your supervisor in terms of status even at your company, whereas my—

EC: If that's up for debate, I mean . . .

F: It's not— Okay, listen. I really need to speak with you about this. I feel like I'm getting the runaround.

EC: No! No, I'm here to help. You called our service line, and you know, I just got back from break, I had a great lunch so I'm feeling good.

F: Okay, I really don't care about whether you had a good lunch or not. I'm also concerned about the first two options on the voice mail, the first one saying peddling influence for the president is in the voice mail, and the second one is specifically for porn stars.

EC: It's not influence, it's insight. And it's not porn stars, it's also models. And it's a typo anyway.

F: What do you mean a typo?

EC: As consultants, my supervisor, who's the only other person who works at this company here, we work out of the office of a taxi maintenance shop in Long Island City.

F: What?

EC: My boss has a unique insight into the president's thinking, so what you pay us for is insight, it's not influence. It's insight. So, do your homework and call us back—

F: All right, you're being very rude, first off. And second, if this is true it sounds to me like your entire company might be fraudulent. If you're not an actual consultancy firm—

EC: We are.

F:—with the proper licensing—

EC: Isn't that state by state?

F: It is state by state. In your state. In New York State.

EC: I'll have to get back to you on that.

F: You should know if you have the proper licensing if you are representing the company.

EC: I assure you that everything we do is in compliance with the law.

F: Well, not this! I'm calling you specifically about something that is not in compliance with the law.

EC: That's up for debate.

F: It's not up for debate. This money was then transferred to three separate bank accounts in Niger and transferred through a third-party holding company to a bank that has a relationship with Iran, which is a violation of the OFAC.

EC: Well, we'll agree to disagree on that.

F: I don't want this to be a relative or subjective conversation. We're talking money and the law, those are objective ideas. Now, I can red flag the transfer and get the feds involved if you like. Or I was trying to work this out privately with you as two bankers to each other. Banker to banker.

EC: Well, I'm not a banker, I'm an intern.

F: What?!

EC: Yeah, I go to Sarah Lawrence. Goooo the Lawrences! Go Larries!

F: Oh, you went to Sarah Lawrence? So did I! Listen, don't worry about it, I'll let this one slide.

EC: Oh wow, Thanks! Bye!

F: Bye!

CALL: ESSENTIAL CONSULTANTS (2/12/2018)

Voice Mail: Hi! You've reached Essential Consultants. The essential consulting company. Press 1 if you want to have insight to the president's thinking. Press 2 if you are an adult film actress or model who needs to keep her mouth shut.

Trump: Hi, uh, this is the guy. This is Denny.

E: Mr. Dennison?

T: Yeah, yeah, this is David Dennison, that's right. It's Dennis Dennison. What is it? Dennis Dennison, right?

E: That's right. Mr. Dennison, we really—

T: It's David.

E: It's David Dennison, sir. That's your name.

T: David Dennison. That's me!

E: Mr. Dennison, um, we've been trying to reach you, uh, we really need you to come down and sign some papers. If you'd rather fax them over or mail them over we could take care of that, too, but we're out on Northern Boulevard.

T: Yeah, yeah, where?

E: We're out on Northern Boulevard in Jackson Heights.

T: Oh, brother. All the way out in Jackson Heights? Listen. I don't use a fax because I got my finger stuck in it once, and then I was afraid they sent my fingerprint over the fax line to somebody else, and that's identity theft. And I don't mail things cause right now apparently I'm banned from using the mail just cause I tried to tell the postmaster general to raise the rates on Amazon! Unbelievable. And now I can't even mail a letter! Not even a postcard.

E: Are you with a senator? Senators have the power of franking—

T: What?!

E: A senator's signature is as good as a stamp.

T: Franken?! I thought we got rid of him! I was going to send a thank-you note to Gillibrand about that. But if you're telling me I don't need to buy stamps I can have Mitch McConnell sign the envelope and I might be a winner. Funnyman Ed McMahon comes to my door and I break down. I say, "Oh My God, Oh My God! No Way!" And he hands me that big check, from the Publisher.

E: We actually do need you to sign some checks as well.

T: The check is from the Publisher, and it's the Publisher who stays in his clearing house and yells "Go Away" at anyone who stops by. But he sends the big checks out. He sends out the big check because he's lonely. Such a big check. It makes me feel like the Incredible Shrinking Woman, starring Lily Tomlin—and the next thing you know I'm on *The Tonight Show* and Johnny loves all my Rally Jokes, like the one about how Me Too makes men have to be more careful about getting what they want. But we'll have a moment of silence, too, because late night died with Johnny Carson. But it wasn't in vain because we lost so many other lives in the Late Night Wars, which is the only war we ever fought over the thing that died.

E: Sir, I don't want to use your real name and I don't want to give too much information over the phone, but it would be very helpful for us and some of our arrangements if you would sign some of the paperwork.

T: And then I get the money?

E: No, you *give* the money.

T: I get the money? I give the money to you?

E: No, you give the money and you get the silence. And we get the papers.

T: Okay, send me the papers.

E: We'll fax it to you.

T: No! My thumb!

CALL: ESSENTIAL CONSULTANTS (4/19/2017)

Essential Consultants: Hello, Essential Consultants! For insight into the president's thinking, press 1. If you're an adult film actress or model who—

(beep beep beep beep beep)

Lwaxana Lust: Hello?

EC: Hello, Essential Consultants, this is Sally, how can I help you?

L: Uh, yeah, hi, um, my name's Lwaxana Lust. My real name's Betty Sanders. I was told to call this number if, um . . . I've had sex with the president?

EC: Okay, great, let me open a case file for you. Let me get your story and some personal information and then we'll either put you in touch with the *National Enquirer,* who might want to buy your story from you and then kill it, or we could just pay you directly to keep your fucking mouth shut.

L: Uh, okay! Um, well, listen, um, I was in California for an adult convention, I'm an adult actress and model, and some people, friends of friends, told me there was a VIP event with transpo and everything, so they brought me to a house north of Calabasas, and I didn't know who I was going to meet, I really didn't, and I, they brought me into a room in the house, it was sort of furnished but mostly empty, I don't know how to describe it.

EC: You were brought to a safehouse for illicit sex?

L: I thought I was going to die.

EC: Oh, we hear that a lot.

L: Hahaha, I'll bet. So they brought me into this room and it was like a viewing room, and I stood in the center and they put a hood on me, and then they pulled the hood off and there was a series of windows, and in each window was a different man bidding for me.

EC: Okay, I'm not sure how Essential Consultants can help you with this . . .

L: Well, Mr. Trump bought me, and so—

EC: Okay, so first things first, we're going to want to refer to him as Mr. Dennison for the remainder of this conversation.

L: Oh, okay. Mr. . . . . Dennison?

EC: Remember. Dennison like venison. Dennison Tower, Dennison Casino. Dennison Steaks. You know.

L: President Dennison. President Dennison's campaign staff brought me from the house to a hotel room, he said he got lonely on the campaign, and so, listen—

EC: This was during the campaign?

L: Uh, no, this was recently.

EC: During the 2020 rallies?

L: He called it a campaign rally.

EC: Yeah, it's all sort of the same thing. The campaign hasn't really stopped. None of this has stopped, it's never going to stop.

L: Well, I don't really follow politics. Anyway, turns out there were four other girls in the room when I was there! And well, look, I know the deal, even though technically I was kidnapped. I wasn't too scared, I was there to do whatever, and you know, he sat down at the edge of the bed, and his little pud was sticking out, you know, his little—I mean, have you ever seen it?

EC: No, but, I mean, I've heard it described dozens, maybe even hundreds of times.

L: It's like there's three balls, you know? It's like, there's not just like a penis, there's like three balls. And one of the balls, well you know, it—it spits! Haha! But, you know, the other two don't. But that one does! So anyway, we did our thing, and we finished, and I said, "Oh my god, I can't wait to tell people I met the president." And he shoved me down onto the bed and pushed a lamp neck onto my throat and said, "Do you want to see tomorrow? Do you want to see tomorrow?" And I was like, "Yes! Yes I do!" and so he pulled the lamp neck off me and we laid down and we watched *Edge of Tomorrow*, which is the real title, not "Tomorrow." It's the one with Tom Cruise and Emily Blunt.

EC: I thought that was called *Live Die Repeat*?

L: Yes, but that was when they released it on DVD, originally called *Edge of Tomorrow* which I think is a better title. Anyway, I didn't get to see how it ended because Mr. Dennison told me to go in the other room and call this number.

EC: Oh, I see. So you're there now.

L: Yeah.

EC: I see. Okay, well, Lwaxana, I just need a couple more pieces of information to give you a quote. Can you tell me your approximate annual salary? And you don't have to include alimony or child support payments if you don't want to.

L: So you said my annual salary?

EC: Yes, we're going to do a credit check on you here and then we're going to quote you your settlement offer.

L: Okay, well my annual salary—obviously you know with the Internet and PornHub and everything it's harder to make a living, but I did a lot of stuff in Romania this year and you don't need to use protection so that's good, you get paid more, so I would say maybe like $80,000?

EC: Okay—

L: Declared income.

EC: Of course. And roughly how much are your monthly expenses?

L: Well, I have two sugar daddies right now, so I'm actually in the black. I actually make $4,000 a month.

EC: Oh, I see. But your rent, and things like that?

L: Yeah, that's all paid for by my sugar daddies.

EC: Oh, that's great. All right, so we're prepared to make you—

L: I'm a sugar baby.

EC: We're prepared to make a personalized settlement offer based on your information. Now this is a limited offer, you can agree to it now, $225,000, paid to you in installments from Essential Consultants. You'll be 1099ed at the end of the year.

L: Oh—wait a minute—I'm sorry—

EC: And all you need to do is shut the fuck up.

L: Okay, okay. I get the last part, but like, 1099, really? That's almost 40 percent of my earnings. Why can't I W2?

EC: Well, no, actually, under the new tax law, you'll be—under the new tax law it's probably better to be an independent contractor or form your own C corporation.

L: Oh trust me, I've got my own C corporation.

EC: Oh, I hear ya, girl!

L: Okay, well, I guess, fine. I guess I'll take the 225. I mean, I'd love to see Mr. Trump again. He promised me that there was a possible opening for chief of staff at the White House. I mean, Mr. Dennison—I mean President Dennison—I mean David—I—

EC: It's okay. I know you're new at this. Well, if you continue sleeping with him, just keep calling us back.

L: Okay, well, wow. Probably not, but, I mean, that's nice of you. And the *Enquirer,* that's pretty big. How do you keep this going? This whole operation sounds like a nightmare that's gonna end really poorly.

EC: I hear you, but it's been fine so far, fingers crossed!

L: Well, thanks a lot! I'm glad to be a part of Essential Consultants!

EC: Is there anything else I can do to assist you on this call?

L: No, I'm totally satisfied with everything, thank you.

EC: Can we use your testimonial on our website?

L: Of course! Of course!

EC: Thank you!

L: No, no. Really. Thank *you.*

EC: Would you mind taking a brief survey after you hang up?

L: Sure, absolutely!

EC: Nice talking to you!

L: You too!

EC: Take care, 'bye!

(beep)

Recording: Hi, and thank you for agreeing to take the brief survey. Do you remember the name of the associate you spoke to? Was it Michael Cohen or Sally?

L: Uh, Sally.

R: Did Sally refer to you by name?

L: Yes.

R: Did Sally thank you for calling Essential Consultants?

L: Yes, she did. Is this a message? Can I record something?

EC: It's just Sally still!

L: What?! Sally! I didn't recognize your voice at all!

EC: I know, I changed it!

L: Wow! I guess I'll leave my message with you. I've never felt more comfortable and taken care of after a kidnapping and coercive sexual experience, so I just want you to know that you always have a loyal customer with me, and I hope they're paying you well over there!

EC: I'm an intern.

L: What?!

CALL: ESSENTIAL CONSULTANTS (6/2/2017)

Voice Mail: Hi! You've reached Essential Consultants. The essential consulting company. Press 1 if you want to have insight to the president's thinking. Press 2 if you are an adult film actress or model who needs to keep her mouth shut.

Trump: ONE! Hello?

EC: Essential Consultants, providing insights into the president's thinking since 2016.

T: Okay, all right, honey. Listen. It's Davis Dennison or Dennis Dennison or whatever the hell my name is. And I wanted to know if anyone's called the number and what requests I have this week. Cause right now I'm setting up a blockage of guatter . . . cutter . . . wutter. I'm blocking them. I've got a big blockage, and I need to know where the money's coming from, honey. Who am I supposed to be talking to next. Those Arabs said they were going to make sure I was safe, just like they promised Dean Martin in *Cannonball Run 2*!

EC: Yes, sir. Well, I'm happy to report that the House of Saud has made a very generous purchase of insight this week. We have a prescription drug company that we're about to close a deal with—

T: What's the drug?

EC: They're purchasing a lot of insight and a—

T: What's the drug?!

EC: A third company that wants to merge with a certain cable company, they've also purchased a few reams of insight that might affect your decision making this week.

T: Wow. Okay, so when do I get the money?

EC: After you leave the presidency, sir.

T: What?! Wait a minute! I thought this whole thing is that it's like an ATM! I need money!

EC: What do you need money for? Do you want to talk to Mr. Cohen?

T: Yeah, is he there?

EC: He's shaking down a cabdriver for his monthly medallion payment.

T: There we go, that's my Cohen.

Cohen: I'll see you tomorrow, you sonofabitch!

T: Michael?!

C: Mr. President. Dennis. Uh. Boss.

T: No, Dennis! Listen to me. First off, you get the money from that cab guy?

C: Yeah, he owed me $75.

T: Get all the tips, too?

C: Yeah, well I skim the tips, yeah.

T: You gotta skim the tips. Always skim the tips with the cabbies. Cause they're always holding on to more than they say! I know how people tip now. Listen, Michael. I thought this whole thing was I was going to be able to take money out in the interim.

C: Well, sir, I can't give money to you. I can handle whatever you need.

T: What?

C: I can handle anything you need in the interim. I can't get you the money.

T: Listen, the midterms are coming up, I gotta make things happen. I gotta be able to pay people off. And I know if I get the money from this account, then I can call you, give you the money, and then you can put it into some secret account!

C: Just leave your bank account out of it, sir. Don't worry, I've got a handle on this.

T: Tell me the password to my bank account.

C: I can't tell you the password.

T: I tried to do a reset and they told me I was fraudulent.

C: Yes, sir. Well, they're probably not used to getting calls from the White House.

T: Well, anyway. I'm really excited about all of these payoffs. I think we've got a lot of great business to do. And wait until everyone finds out that we've been actually doing tons of business with Iran!

C: Sir, the contributions have been made, the commissions have been paid, and the money will be waiting for you after you exit the presidency.

T: Michael, I'm not going anywhere. Not until I die. And they'll drop the flag and everyone will say "We miss Trump."

C: Well, then it'll go to your kids, sir. The Trump Organization will carry on long after you've sadly passed away.

T: The boys? Those walking abortions?! No way. I'm not letting them get dime one. Eric will spend it all on cotton candy. Don Jr. will just go to Africa and find dead animals and pay people to say that they were hunting him and he turned the tables on them. Even Ivanka, she doesn't need another pair of tits. She had a baby, that's it for her. Our only hope, cause there is another, is to do serious facial reconstruction surgery on Tiffany, give her the face I leave behind.

C: You want to take your face off of your corpse and put it onto Tiffany?

T: Listen. Before I die, make sure that you put that in my will or whatever, okay? That when I pass on, you take my face off and put it on Tiffany's face. And then put Tiffany's face on my face, and bury it! Remember, Michael! Face. Off. Face. Off.

C: Okay, I made those notes, sir. I'll—

T: Yeah! You got it down? Listen, Michael. If only people knew we were doing all these deals with North Korea and Iran while I'm talking tough the entire time. I mean, the Iranians must be laughing at the fact that I withdrew from the nuclear deal while I'm receiving large sums of money from them through back channels! I mean, the whole thing's a fun joke, you know what I mean? I mean look at what we did with the Chinese! All I needed to do was a big public tough talking, and meanwhile in the backdrop, all of our chief negotiators and people who do backchannel third party deals arranged for China to buy over 250 billion dollars of new product from the United States. Cause we're fleecing everybody! And now I'm bailing out their companies! It's perfect. Also, maybe you should transfer me to line 2. I got another girl I gotta pay.

WHICH HUNT IS WITCH

TRANSCRIPT: MUELLER TESTIMONY PREPARATION (7/28/2018)

Trump: All right, I'm ready, guys. Let's hit it because I am going to mop the floor with this Mueller. I am so ready to meet with this guy.

Attorney: Well sir, we're actually doing everything we can to stop you from meeting him, but in case you get subpoenaed, we should prepare just like we tried to do with mock debates with Hillary—we never did them because you slept in—but we wanted to mock debates before the debates. It's good to go over some of the things we can expect him to talk about.

T: All I'm saying is bring him on because I'm gonna totally charm him. At the end of this he is gonna say, "Trump, can we be friends? Can we be friends? I'm so sorry. I'm so sorry."

A: We certainly hope that happens, sir. The first question that they sent over was—

T: Are we in it now?

A: We're in it, sir.

T: Okay, now. Now I'm ready.

A: So these are the questions that they sent that you can expect to have them ask you if you sit down with the Mueller team.

T: Yes.

A: What did you know about Sally Yates's meetings with Mr. Flynn?

T: Sally Yates—all I know is this. She sat down with Flynn and she said, "You gotta tell me what's going on, you gotta tell me about the collusion." And Flynn's a good guy, he's got a great son, and he's a real hero, and he fought for this country, okay? He fought for this country. Obama had him, and Obama didn't have a problem with him. And Sally Yates, she says to him, "What's this with the collusion, what did you do?" and she goes, "We gotcha. We got ya dead to rights." And Flynn says, "Sorry, I don't know what you're talking about," which is true! And then apparently they said to him, "Well, we have money that you got paid," and that money, yeah, he got paid that money, and that money was for services that had nothing to do with the campaign. Nothing to do with the campaign. Did it come from people who met with the campaign? Of course it did. Did it come from people who had just spoken to me or my son within the last three days? Yeah! But just because two people—I mean— that's like saying—hold on—excuse me—hold on—that's like saying you run into some guy and you talk to him about, you know, you say to him, "Hey, are you gonna rob the bank," and he says, "Yeah, I'm going to rob the bank," and you go, "Okay," and then like ten minutes later, he goes and robs the bank! You don't have anything to do with that, unless you pick him up and drive him away, and even then, what did you know? I was just the getaway guy!

A: Sir, our legal team encourages you to say you do not recall.

T: Okay, let's try it again.

A: What do you know about Sally Yates's meetings with Mr. Flynn?

T: I do not recall the first time I heard about Sally Yates and Michael Flynn. But I recall the second time I heard about it, and it was really terrible because Michael got himself into some hot water with money from the Russians and let's face it, there were people I was doing business with as well. And we were trying to get that hotel built, and they said, "Listen, we'll make you president, and if you become president then you can change all these tax laws and you can change trade and you can lay off on the Russians." Which we should do. And sanctions, we gotta get rid of these sanctions. Why are we sanctioning anybody? Last time I checked, a sanction is an endorsement. I sanction that, I sanction the Russians. So in that sense, I was helping everybody! And so, Michael got a kickback, big deal. We get the hotel and we'll roll out of there. Oh boy, we're in that hotel, and Michael's got a job as a bellboy!

A: All right, again, sir, we'd just encourage you to say you didn't know anything about Sally Yates meeting with Mr. Flynn except for—

T: But I know Sally Yates. She worked for the Clintons and she was a total jerk!

A: All right, sir. They're going to ask you about your dinner with James Comey. So what was the purpose of your dinner on January 27 with Mr. Comey, and what was said at the dinner?

T: Well, first off, we had the White House chef prepare an incredible meal. And we released a dummy menu to the public. It was like a fancy menu. But I knew, Comey's an FBI guy, and he'd want to eat like it was a stakeout! So, I got two big Italian submarine gyros and—with all the meat and all the fixins. And two bottles of Coca-Cola—Diet Coke for me. And a big bunch of chips in the middle. And I said, "This is like a stakeout!" And I even put the seats like they were next to each other in a car so we could sit and have a real conversation, just two top cops. And so, what was the purpose? To tell Comey to lay off the Russia investigation. Because this guy is all up in my business! And the fact is, there's a lot of stuff I have to hide! Because let's face it. I wasn't on the up-and-up before I came into the White House and I had a lot of weird business dealings that even I don't know about because Michael handled most of that stuff, I just gave him the money, and he handled it, and he handled it, and I got my money, and that's all that mattered. So I said, "Comey, lay off. Don't you want to stay the FBI director? Cause I'm gonna fire you if you don't do this." And then, you know, I wanted to know if they had the tape, because, if they got me with the women pissing on the bed, that's bad news. But at the same time, I might want to beat it to it. I wish I got a tape of it, because I want to pleasure myself. Pleasure myself to the tape.

A: All right, so the legal team is encouraging you to say you didn't know Mr. Comey very well and you thought by having dinner with him you could improve your working relationship.

T: I knew who he was! He was so great with the Hillary thing, then he wasn't great, then he was great again, and I didn't care about having a relationship with him. I wanted the guy to stop investigating Russia because we had serious entanglements with the Russian Mafia, illegal shell banks, and a bunch of other bad players that we had been moving our money around with for over twenty-five years!

A: We don't want to mention that, sir.

T: Okay . . . so should I just say that I have a relationship with just the Russians?

A: No, I would just say that you wanted to have dinner with Comey for work reasons.

T: But what about the pleasure tape?

A: We don't want to bring that up, sir.

T: But I wanna know!

A: Why did you hold Jeff Sessions's resignation until May 31, 2017, and with whom did you discuss it?

T: I held it because I wanted—listen, first off, I wanted to see if Jeff would turn around and do the right thing, okay? He should have never recused himself from the Russia investigation. It's the whole reason I put him in there! I mean, this guy is a total drip, okay? And he's easy to pay off. Let me say that. One of the first people with me on the campaign. And I thought Jeff would be very easy. And Jeff turned out to be very hard. For such a little guy with such big ears? I mean he's like the white Obama. And I said to him, I said, "Listen to me, Jeff. Don't resign. Cause if you resign, I will take you down like a house of cards." I mean let's face it, this guy is so linked with our campaign. He knew all about the Russian money transfers, he knew about meeting with the consultants. He knew about the Trump Tower that my son went to and was calling me from time to time to let me know what info the Russians had and how they could help give the hack and send the emails and get the election where we needed it. So I said to Jeff, "That's all going to come out and you're going to be totally ruined. Totally ruined. But if you stick with me, I promise, I'll keep quiet." And then what does the jerk do, he recuses himself, but then stays in office! That means then I'm screwed because I can't say anything and the guy's got no power.

A: The legal team's encouraging that instead you say you have confidence in Mr. Session's role as Attorney General so you didn't accept his resignation.

T: I'll remember that.

A: Next. When you went to Russia in 2013, did you communicate with—

T: That was a great trip.

A:—did you communicate with representatives of the Russian government or Russian real estate investors?

T: Yeah! I talked to all kinds of guys. But the thing is, we did it really really smart. Very smart. We did it very smart. So, what we would do is meet in the hotel lobby, and then we would move to a second location because usually there would be a tail car. So once we lost the tail car by switching inside some parking garage, we'd end up in an apartment—usually some Russian nobody—I mean, these people's faces when you come in the door! "Don't kill me, don't kill me! Don't kill me, don't kill me!" And we say "just be quiet, just let us meet in your living room. Nobody wants to kill you." We were very nice. And we met with a lot of guys. Different bankers, real estate developers, and of course the people who are friends of Putin. Big guys. And these are big guys. And I know them all. I know them all. I know every one of them. And we have a great relationship with them. I know the big guys, big money guys. And you know Putin and I did the video chat, which was incredible.

A: The legal team's advising you say you did not meet any representatives from the Russian government and you were just there to do the Miss Universe pageant.

T: Well, that was another thing, because you know, Miss Universe was unbelievable that year. The age of consent in Russia is sixteen or fourteen, I can't remember. So, you know, we go to the dressing room and all those beautiful girls are in there, you know, and they got their tops off, some of them got their bottoms off, and it's beautiful, you know, and you're seeing these young girls right at their prime, you know, right when they're supposed to be having babies. And that's the thing young girls don't understand. You're supposed to be having babies when you're fourteen or fifteen. Because then the body bounces back. All these women are having babies when they're thirty-seven or thirty-eight—of course you're gonna look like a slug afterward. But when you have them young, and then you stay young—and that's what they don't understand.

A: So, we—the legal team actually doesn't mind if you want to continue that train of thought because it doesn't incriminate you in any way.

T: Then I'm finished.

A: Fine. What involvement did you have concerning changes to the Republican platform about arming the Ukraine?

T: Well, the first thing was that the platform was too low! And I said, "How are the cameras going to catch me if I'm walking out on such a low platform?" So, you know, I'm in construction, and I understand how a stage is built. So I said, "Let's get these Ukrainian guys in here, they know how to lift the stage for cheap." I got a great deal on it, I only paid forty cents on the dollar to get the job done. And it was a beautiful stage, it was a beautiful convention, one of the great conventions.

A: If Mueller lets you get away with that answer, sir, that would be a real boon for us. Next: what do you know about a 2017 meeting in Seychelles involving Erik Prince in the United Arab Emirates?

T: Well, that Chili's is incredible because it's still got the nacho platter and the buffalo wings and even the potato skins! And a lot of the Chili's don't offer that anymore, they went way more Tex-Mex. And you can get margaritas in everything! I mean, I don't drink, but I thought it was a really great restaurant.

A: What communications did you have with Michael Cohen, Felix Sater, and others about Russian real estate developments during the campaign?

T: I mean, we talked about all kinds of business deals. Michael, you know, all these guys, we do all the business deals, and you know, of course Don Jr.—the not original Trump—he's, you know, in charge of the day-to-day but it's very important because we have a lot of property deals, and Michael of course has a very large slush fund with a company called Essential Consultants and that's where I'd put all my money, I would give it to Michael and of course he'd do the payouts, and hold my money for me, especially any money that came from what we called "bad actors." Bad actors. And the bad actors, you know, let's face it. The same way that I don't want people knowing I know Steven Seagal? I don't want people to know that I know bad actors on the world stage either. But of course, they're all very good.

CALL: BLOCKED NUMBER TO ROBERT MUELLER
12/10/2017

Mueller (Recording): Hi, you've reached Bob Mueller on my personal line. Can't come to the phone right now, so leave me a message and I'll get back to you as soon as I can.

Unknown Caller: You can't tell who this is. You have no idea. But let me tell you, you better lay off Trump. You hear me? Because you got something real bad coming your way if you don't take your Herman Munster head and turn around and go back to the FBI and find someone like Hillary Clinton to go after because that guy's innocent, and he doesn't like the way you've been treating him, and you've never even sat down to have dinner with him or you'd be saying Trump's a great guy!

CALL: BLOCKED NUMBER TO ROBERT MUELLER
5/11/2018

Mueller (Recording) Hi, you've reached Bob Mueller on my personal line. Can't come to the phone right now, so leave me a message and I'll get back to you as soon as I can.

Unknown Caller: Oh, boy. Okay. Hi, this is David Dennison. Uh. Listen to me. You don't know who this is, really. It could be anyone. But it's a blocked number, so how will you ever be able to tell? Now, let me tell you. Many people are saying that you're going too hard on Trump, and what you need to do is lay off, and then he'll talk to you! He wants to talk to you, but he wants to talk to you about all kinds of fun things. Like what's going on on *The Voice*, or can you believe that *Big Bang Theory* got two more seasons? There's plenty of fun things to talk about. But my friend Sean Hannity says I should stop talking to you or calling you! I mean, not my friend—I don't know—guhh—goodbye!

CALL: BLOCKED NUMBER TO ROBERT MUELLER
6/7/2018

Mueller: Uh, hello.

Trump: Hello?

M: Who is this?

T: Don't you worry about that. What are you doing?

M: I'm not going to answer that. Do you know who you're talking to?

T: Yeah, this is Robert Mueller, right?

M: This is Robert Mueller.

T: Okay . . . you don't know who this is, though, right?

M: Well, I have a guess. And if you are who I think you are, you really shouldn't be calling me.

T: You gotta lay off Trump, you hear me?

M: What?

T: You gotta lay off Trump. Never mind who this is. Back off, buddy.

M: Really?

T: Yeah! You better back off.

M: Should I really?

T: You should definitely, totally end the investigation. It's a total witch hunt and I'm telling you right now this guy's got very powerful friends. And I wouldn't want something to happen to you.

M: Fine. Maybe I will lay off.

T: Wow, really?

M: No.

T: What? What was that?

M: It was a joke. Actually, I'm gonna lay on even more because you called me. Fuck you.

T: Well—excuse me—fuck you, buddy, you can go fuck yourself. Go fuck your mother, okay? Go fuck your mother. Go fuck your mother. You fuck your mother. You—you're a motherfucker.

M: Hey, come say that to my face, you asshole.

T: I will say it to your face. I'll put my fist to your face. You understand me? Not that it needs any help.

M: Get off. Fuck you.

T: Listen to me, you pig.

M: You can't do shit, you can't do shit. Fuck you.

T: You can eat shit. You eat shit out of a bowl like a dog. Everybody knows it.

M: You can't do anything, fuck you.

T: Really? Yeah? You'll see if I come testify. If I come testify you'll be totally screwed, you understand that?

M: Oh, so it is you. It's the president.

T: No, I'm not saying that. I'm just saying if I came and testified. I didn't say anything. You can't get me, Mueller.

M: Well, who are you to come testify? Who the fuck are you?

T: Who the fuck are *you*? Why don't *you* testify!

M: I'm Robert Mueller!

T: Oh, I got you to say your name, doofus!

M: Well, I knew my name. I said I was me when you called, asshole.

T: Yeah, well, whatever! You revealed yourself.

M: Oh, "whatever," oh nice, oh good comeback, oh whatever. Fuck you.

T: You know what? Eat shit. Eat shit, stinkbird. I'm never talking to you. I'm not listening to Jeff Sessions. I'm never talking to you, you understand me?

M: Good, I don't want you to talk to me. I don't want to talk to you either.

T: You don't want to talk to me? I don't wanna talk to you!

M: Well you called me!

T: Well you called—no—yeah, sure, but that's cause I wanted you to talk, and you did, so I control you!

M: You don't control me.

T: I totally control you. You're my puppet.

M: You're the puppet.

T: No, you're the puppet. You're my puppet.

M: All right, I know that's you, Trump. Fuck you. You're going down. You're going down. Sorry.

T: Only thing you're going down on is your mom. You're going down on a dog. You're going down on—go to the zoo! And go eat out a giraffe, you pervert!

M: You're the pervert. You're the one paying off Playmates, cheating on your wife.

T: No! No!

M: Horny for your daughter, pissing on sheets. Piss freak.

T: At least I'm getting laid, okay? At least I'm getting laid.

M: I'm getting plenty laid.

T: You getting laid? Yeah right, with a head like that?

M: Believe me, I'm getting plenty laid. Fuck you.

T: Oh, fuck you. Listen, let me tell you something. I see more pussy in a day than you see in a lifetime, okay? And that's if you worked in a cat rescue center.

M: We'll see. We'll see about that. Fuck you.

T: Yeah, fuck you, buddy! Why don't you come over here and say that to me!

M: Okay, I'm coming over.

T: Yeah, you coming over?

M: I'm coming over right now.

T: Yeah, 1600 Pennsylvania Asshole Avenue.

M: Yeah, so it's the White House, huh?

T: Yeah? No, no. No. No. No. No. No. I live—uh, uh, ah—no, there's another house right there, its $1600^{1}/_{2}$.

M: All right, I'll meet you there. I'll meet you there in an hour and a half.

T: Yeah, I'll meet you. I'll be out front. Out in front.

M: I'll see you there.

T: Yeah, I'll see you there. I'll see you there. You better be prepared for a bruising, buddy.

M: I'll kick your ass.

T: Yeah, whatever.

M: Fuck you.

T: Fuck off. You get off the phone.

M: Asshole.

Archivist's Note

I was fired today. Or I should say my position was eliminated. The library project was being blackballed effective immediately. I was to gather my materials and return them to the White House without delay. I saw more than a little satisfaction on John Kelly's face when he gave me the news. He said that he never thought I belonged there. I didn't know how to tie a tie like a gentleman and my corduroys gave a distasteful squeak when I shuffled in my armchair, but he wished me the best of luck back in Florida. I asked to speak to the president but Kelly told me that would not be possible. So I went back to my hotel in a daze and started packing my bags. I had seen the Garden, and now I was being expelled. I stuffed my papers in a mailer, sorted the cans for recycling, and picked the tissues off the floor. I was just about to check my bank balance on my cracked smartphone when the screen flickered and the phone rang from a blocked number. I paused for a moment then answered. To my surprise, I heard the voice of the president. "I want you to publish. Publish everything right now."

I was stunned. I asked him why the change. He said he had talked to Rudy and that they were taking a new tack. "Get it all out there," he said, "get our story out first, get ahead of it. We're fucked. We're fucked. They can't do this to us. They can't do this to Trump. We're fucked." For the first time, I heard something in his voice that sounded pathetic. How had I never noticed it before? He was afraid. He was afraid of everything. In a flash I couldn't believe what a fool I'd been: This is the guy I was going to give up my life for? This is the guy who got between me and my wife? My stomach turned with a familiar disgust. I dutifully told the president that I had reviewed some of the material and that he might object to some of it being public. He said Rudy said that didn't matter. Rudy said Publish everything. So that was it.

I told the president he would see his Library in print exactly as I'd promised him. It would be tremendous. He didn't seem to remember why we were on the phone. America's Mayor was muttering in the background about attorney-client privilege. I glanced down at my notes for the interview I planned to end the volume with, and it occurred to me what Trump and his rabid base have in common: They will stop at nothing to get what they want, but they are just too dumb to get anything done. At least I hope that's true. I guess we'll find out.

Kelsey Nelson

THE FUTURE

Russian: What do you want.

Trump: This is President Trump calling. Is this one of my incredible trolls?

R: No, no, no, no, no. Do not call this number. Lose number.

T: I know it's hard to accept, you getting a call from Trump. A troll getting a call from the president. So I expect you to be very surprised! But the truth is that we want—we have a big day coming up tomorrow and I wanted to call and give you, what do they call it—uh, a pep talk, something. Raise your spirits. A good boost for morale.

R: Please, we cannot discuss, sir. I would hang up the phone but if I disrespect for you, then they make my family disappear.

T: I know, trust me. I get it. I know, I know, I know. You're looking for a raise. You work hard, you don't want to be bothered. We don't have the money right now to help you out but I promise you after the midterm, big bonuses all around.

R: Sir, please. Please. I do not want to hang up on you because of what they will do to my family if I am rude to you. Please, please, sir. The less you say, the better. And there's no guarantee. We should not know each other.

T: I don't want to know anything, okay? I don't want to know what you're going to do, I don't want to know about your access to the voter rolls or how it was far more deep and far more integrated into our voting system than anyone anticipated. I don't want to know anything. So. Tell me the plan for tomorrow.

R: Well, sir. We have access to many systems. We have access to data. As they know, we have the ability to change some data in a way that nobody will notice, just as we did several years ago. This is the most I can say.

T: Where are you? Are you in Russia?

R: We are in Siberia.

T: We are?

R: I am.

T: Where am I?

R: I don't know.

T: Good. Let's keep it that way. You passed the first test. Now, it's very important to me that nobody know anything, okay? And also, let's face it. The best work you guys did in 2016 was using our own social networks and shallow media literacy to plant stories that exacerbated fissures in American culture that have existed for centuries to motivate people to vote differently, really not even doing anything illegal!

R: That was a big part of it. Pretty cool, right?

T: So incredible. America is so weak. They're a bunch of weakies. But we can't tell anybody that. We know that. We need to be strong, like Russia! Right? Right? Am I right?

R: Yes, we are strong, sir. You are strong. You're very strong man. You're strong like a Russian.

T: Too bad you're a troll. You have a hard time because you live under a bridge, you can't get good cell service down there, plus you still gotta get coins from everybody who passes!

R: No sir. Sir, this is a confusion from language.

T: A confusion from language? All I know—

R: Our language is confused. We are the uh, cyber—we work on the computer.

T: Troll lives in computer . . . troll lives in computer! How do you make the computer work?

R: Well, um. We use a blade server farm here, and the virtualization, and multiple terminals that can be made from stock hardware.

T: Okay . . . How do I get my gmail—

R: We are not worried about your gmail, sir.

T: I'm worried about it!

R: But as you know, many voting systems in your country in many states are running on technology from twenty years ago. You have Window 95 computers running voting touch screens that are backed by an Access database that isn't even encrypted. You take security at your casinos and deli ATMs more seriously. Even with good security, electronic voting solves no problems with paper ballots but introduces many many new ones.

T: So embarrassing, so unbelievable that the United States fails so incredibly with old voting machines. But you know what I say. I say, everyone says to me, "Mr. Trump, Mr. Trump, please! We need to fix the voting machines, we need to fix the voter rolls, the system is broken. And I say, leave it that way! Who cares! It's the only way I'm going to get reelected or the Republicans are going to keep the house. That's for sure. It's working for me. And by the way, Blue Wave? More like blue little trickle out of someone's peepee. There's no way. I mean, we're talking—this is a prostate-choked wave. There's no way. There's gonna be no wave. The only thing we're going to be doing is waving goodbye to the Democrats when they lose tomorrow on election day. And we'll be grateful, believe me.

R: Well, we accept your gratitude, sir. But if you'll excuse me, we should get back to work.

T: Listen to me. Before you go. Can you hack—I have a list of the top ten famous actresses who I'd like to see sexy naked selfies from. Could you hack them? Can I have them?

R: Oh, we have them already. We have everybody's everything.

T: Well, could you send me Jessica Alba, Suzanne Somers—I know, it seems weird, but I can't get her out of my mind. She'll always be Chrissy to me. And I'll send the rest of the list over—

R: Sir, I should say, we are very busy tonight and tomorrow. This is night before election. We cannot be diverting our resources to sending nudie pictures.

T: Well, that's fine. I'll just rely on my old-fashioned spank bank. Can't hack that, baby. Not yet! Unless they can put a chip in your brain. Can they put a chip in your brain?

R: No, I can't.

T: But can somebody?

R: Maybe. Ivan? *[Russian speech]*

Ivan: Yes.

R: He says maybe.

T: Wow!

R: *Nastrovia!*

T: Nostradamus!

INTERVIEW: 2020 RE-ELECTION PLAN

Kelsey: Sir, you're the only president that's released his presidential library at the end of his first term.

Trump: It's incredible, isn't it? They said it couldn't be done. They said we couldn't do anything we did.

K: But you did it.

T: But will they say it?

K: No.

T: And there's so much more. So much. Twenty-twenty. The vision.

K: What is your vision for 2020?

T: It's going to be very tough. Very tough. I've met with some of the top minds. Some of the great minds, political minds, minds that are the great strategists, makers of the political landscape. The inside guys. And listen, I was fighting against these guys. These were the people I was running against. But then, you gotta do it. You gotta turn and make them work for you. And 2020's tough. It's not going to be easy. Not gonna be easy at all. The Democrats—okay, listen. A lot of weak Democrats, but they're gonna gain. And they're tough, very tough. And there's a lot of great people that can run. A lot of tough Democrats.

K: What about Kamala Harris?

T: You got Kamala Harris. Obama. Clinton. I mean she's Obama Clinton.

K: What about John Kerry?

T: I mean, John Kerry would be crazy if he ran. That guy'd be crazy if he ran. He already got the swift boat. And the swift boat's gonna come back. Swift boat's gonna pull right into the harbor, go toot toot, and John Kerry's gonna get on it and he's gonna sail away.

K: What about Joe Biden?

T: You got Joe Biden—this guy. I'd drop him. I'd sock him in the jaw and he'd drop like a sack. Biden could be in there, but he's old news. He's old news. You got Kirsten Gillibrand. Young, blond, sexy, okay? You got that governor, Andy Cuomo. Okay? People in New York don't even like him. And that thing with the mayor—those two don't even like each other. And that's going to be tough. I get along with all the mayors. Every mayor loves me—even John Mayer! And he's the mayor of music. But we're gonna fight, and it's going to be tough. And going into November 2020, who knows what's going to happen. I'm the only one who's saying the election might be stolen, I said it before and then it was! And we don't know what's going to happen—the Russians, if this hacking is true, if this hacking is happening, and Hillary, she's the one who asked the Russians to hack. Hillary's the one who set this all up. She's the one who took money from the Russians and gave the money to the Russians. Uranium 1, Uranium 2, Uranium 3! Uranium 4—Miami Patrol. We got them all. Uranium 5: Johnny 5's Alive! It's all there. And the truth is, is if you trace the money back to the Clintons, this is what most people don't know about 2016. Russia, Russia—Russia's working with the Clintons! They're all connected to the Democrats. The Democrats are the ones who hacked the election. They threw it to me out of spite. But we need to have a good relationship with Russia. We should have a great relationship with Russia. We need to get Russia settled down. And they understand that they're dealing with a tough guy now. But the Democrats have the hacking tools now, so who knows what's going to happen. They say they don't hack, but since they did—and we know they did—they might do it again because if they don't, we will. I don't think it's gonna look good, to be honest with you. I don't think it's gonna look good. And I believe, coming into that election, it's very difficult, and I don't know what the result's gonna be. And the result could be tough, and we're gonna have to hang in there. And that's the problem.

K: But you do expect to win, sir?

T: I think we have a tough—I don't know what's going to happen. I can't say anything—I'd like to win. I think we should win. But who knows what the result is. We could all be waking up not knowing what anything's happening. The truth of the matter is we could be looking at the Democrats saying, "We won, we won" but we know they didn't win. And that election day, there's so many irregularities. And the truth is we need the Xe. We need the Xe and the Academi and the Amway, the good old Blackwater boys. And those boys, they were tough. They fought in Fallujah, they fought all over the world. And they're private. They're private military. Which we love. We love the private. We love the private. And the private's very good for us. And so, and I personally think, and I'd hate to do it, I'd hate to do it—I'd use the National Guard if I could, but I can't. They say you can't do it. And I wish I could. I thought when you're president you could say what you wanted to do. But you can't. And so, we'll have to have the private. And the private Blackwater, they'll be there at the voting polls making sure that the right people are voting, that people with the proper papers are voting, that there aren't the radical Antifa and Unclefa, all of them are there. Unclefa, Antifa, we know they're coming, and our guys will show them the door. But the election's really important, and it's all about the campaign. And all about the great rallies and the campaign and making sure we get up there and remember—we reach the people. And we reach the people with the cyber and the computer. These computer guys! And these computer guys know what they're doing. And they've got all the research. You know, we did great on the Facebook, and we did great on the Twitter. We do the hits and we make the hits and people get the views. And we're getting all the views. It's unbelievable! You look at the views and we're getting more views than anybody. And everyone's viewing us. And you get the data and the data points and the data points in one direction and it says who are the voters and what are they thinking. We got the Jesus guy who wants to lower the taxes. And we got the Jesus guy who he wants to let immigrants in, and we gotta separate them. We don't want to talk to the Jesus guy who likes the immigrants. We want the Jesus guy who's got the tax cuts. We need—listen—we got an old lady, and there's so many old ladies who aren't good on the iPad but they love Trump. These old ladies, they go, "Trump! We want Trump! We want Trump! Trump saves the guns!" And we get the teachers. And some teachers are old ladies! And those old ladies have guns. And we send them all a message. And it's incredible. The cyber, and the computer, and all the information we're gathering and we're going to put it to work. And if we lose the election or if the election is muddy, cause I don't like to say lose, cause I never like the word lose. But if we win poorly, and the Democrats are saying, "We won, we won, we're the victory. We're the president now," we have an incredible database and it's a database. And this gives us—and I'll tell you, I was talking to Erik Prince the other day and he says, "We got a great plan." And I'll tell you the plan. Hannity and Judge Jeanine Pirro, they have the plan. We're gonna be under siege. The Democrats lying about the win, and we're gonna use the data. Who are the counties, where are the police? And the police that support us. And the people on the ground. The true members of the MAGA world, the MAGA community—and there's so many of them. And we're gonna organize them and we're gonna use this data to reach out to them and say, "Hold strong, hold firm, cause I'm not going anywhere. I will stay by you and defend you to the defense of the forefathers' constitutional right to stay with your arms and keep your towns." And I will say, "Don't give up your town. Don't give it up to these liars. It's corrupt, and the traitors have taken over our country and only I can save it." And then we send the Blackwater boys to the other towns and we have it all. And we have the everything. And I've met a lot of local cops, a lot of good local cops and they're with us. And they're gonna say no. And what is a country but made up of towns and cities. And it's the towns that matter. The sanctuary cities, where the fake votes come from, have the immigrants. The cities are holding immigrants. And we need to surround those cities. That'll be the first thing we need to do. Send the people out of the towns with their guns, which is their Second Amendment right, to protect against the illegals and the traitors and the MS-13. And let's face it, these cities have become foreign countries! They're not even American anymore. The truth is that the cities aren't American but the towns are. And when these Democrats and these liberals who live in these cities and are with the illegals and against the law, they're no longer American cities. Don't we want the big cities? We want the big cities. Everyone in these small towns dreams of going to these cities. But they can't. Because they're hated. Because the liberal elites and global bankers who live in these cities, they look down on them. They look down on them. So we do the Ferguson. The Ferguson but for us. And we need to occupy it. And we need to take the best of Fallujah, the best of Ferguson, all the great people who served in those terrible moments, put them together and make sure we're on the ground. And this is a ground war, folks. It's a ground war. Don't ever forget that. This is a ground war. City to city, building to building, taking people and reminding them of who's in charge. And that could last, for who knows. Who knows. I say the election will not be settled until we find out exactly what happened with the hacking of the 2020 election and how the Democrats stole it. And if it takes ten years, if it takes twenty, if it takes eighty years. Whatever it takes. It might take a century to figure it out. But we must stay in charge to keep normalcy. Normalcy. To keep things running and flowing and keep it safe. And we must be safe. The best safeness. And who provides better safety than the blue lives and the Blue Lives Matter. And that's what matters. We can't allow Black Panthers roaming free. It's fun as a movie, but not fun in real life. And if they don't like it, they can go to Waka-waka-tata, or whatever that place is. Their invisible city filled with blacks.

K: Sir, it sounds to me like you're saying in the event of a loss in 2020, you're going to question the results of the election?

T: I'm not questioning everything. Or anything. What I'm saying is that it's already taken. The election's already stolen. And it's just a matter now of seeing how they do it. It's illegitimate already. It's an illegitimate result. And if it's an illegitimate result, I need to stay there to protect the people. Cause remember, I'm outside politics. I am not politics. And when you don't have politics, that's how you get things done. And if a politician wins, it's probably because they stole it. And if they stole it, then that means we need to put certain things into effect. The marshall, the law. The different things that matter. Curfew. Things that keep people safe. The Constitution is not a suicide pact. Until it is. That's what Steve Miller told me. And that guy—I mean, he knows a thing or two. Have you ever seen his eyes? They're very beady.

THE END

Epilogue

With the Library heading to press and nothing left for me in the nation's capital, I had some thinking (and drinking) to do, so I booked a roomette on the Silver Meteor train back to West Palm Beach.

I remember riding this train back in 1986, the first time Peg and I separated after I went all-in on Lyndon LaRouche. And it was a Metroliner that brought me home from the Golden State when I concluded my affair with L. Ron Hubbard & Company around the Fourth of July, 1997. I guess a long train trip is my little ritual to check back in with reality after getting carried away before I return home and grovel to my wife (whose present enthusiasm for Nxivm classes is somehow not up for discussion).

The best way to see the country is by train. It jolts you out of city life into the world of the people out there who live next to the train tracks. This is Trump country, and it includes people who live places the train doesn't even go. These people have taken a hard look at the life offered to them by the systems designed and controlled by the educated coastal elite and decided to tell them they can shove it where the sun don't shine. They'd rather obliterate the status quo than find out what humiliations it intends to deliver next. They cry that their heritage is being robbed from them. What do they mean by their heritage? It's hard to describe, but it's definitely white. Who is out to get them? That's also unclear, but people a shade or two darker than them might as well take some lumps while they figure it out.

Now, I know the suburbs went for Trump, too, and those people aren't suffering from quite the same afflictions (unless you count heroin and suicide). Suburban Trump voters are guys (and gals) like me: pulling down six figures but living like they make seven, praying that a well-timed tax cut will make up the difference and using credit cards to keep up with their neighbors in the interim. Nothing bothers them more than the idea that they might have to part with a single dime that would wind up going to the wrong people.

My old friend Donald got elected because the aggrieved white almost-rich teamed up with the aggrieved white almost-poor against the mainstream left whose current pitch is retributive justice for their own aggrieved parties: women, racial minorities, LGBT's (and whatever other ticker symbols are bullish these days). Resentment has become the official language of our culture. Resentful people are retreating to tribalism, shouting that the system has to be destroyed because things are worse than ever, even though it's hard to argue exactly how anyone living in this country is suffering worse today than they were two or three generations ago, much less five or ten. And it also ignores the fact that while the 99% are hashing things out, the truly privileged upper class hedge their bets so their interests are served regardless of who is in power at the moment (even though they were rooting for Jeb!).

While the rich stay above the fray, we rage at each other through our screens for the imaginary audience on the other side, projecting a perfect image of ourselves, brave and strong and righteous. And because we are really none of those things, we defend the illusion by trying to destroy anyone who challenges it. Everyone is shouting, nobody is listening, and the screen doesn't care. Technology that we once thought might take us to the stars has instead created a crisis of self-involvement. Lacking any sense of greater purpose and terrified of silence, we adopt the prepackaged personality sold to us by Fox or MSNBC or Bravo or QVC, or we spend our precious time marketing our own personal brand as product and consumer in the churning 24-hour news cycle we have imported even into our private lives.

In this chaos, a motley coalition has formed to demand that someone just blow the whole thing up. What started fifty years ago as a preference for politicians who were more relatable and informal has evolved to finally elect someone exactly like ourselves. We made manifest a man who reflects us perfectly, the president we deserve: a pompous, racist, lying, woman-hating narcissist who will promise anything to anyone but never deliver. A man who doesn't pay his debts but spends exorbitantly to maintain the illusion of his grandiosity. It isn't that Trump is the beginning of all bad things, or the end, it is that he is the result. He is the culmination of the worst parts of American civilization, with some of the endearing parts thrown in to confuse things. This man is a funhouse mirror of our unraveling civilization.

Television loves him, because you can't help but watch the disaster unfold. The permanent political establishment loves him more because he excuses their sins. If you tortured for Bush or flew drones for Obama, or caged immigrant children for both, you're off the hook now because everyone knows nothing evil ever happened before the election of Donald Trump.

I took a break to chew my steak during dinner service after a stop in Rocky Mount. While I was lost in thought, another passenger had joined my table. I couldn't see his face since he was reading *The Financial Times*. I polished off a fifth little bottle of wine and was motioning for the genial Amtrak waitress's attention when the newspaper slid to the ground. Where the stranger had been, a great crow with seven eyes appeared and spoke to me in a shrill monotone that echoed through the dining car.

"The automobile took you away from the market square. The television took you from your neighborhood. Now the phone takes you out of your own life completely. Space and time collapse until you're completely alone, bathed in light. Hell is here on earth and Lucifer is in your pocket, spying on you so he can give you exactly what you want."

"What are you?" I exclaimed, covering my face. The great crow just stared. "What would you have me do?"

"I don't know," the crow said, pecking at a tuna sandwich. "Invest in public infrastructure? Community colleges, libraries, roads, bridges, airports, that kind of thing has pretty universal support, right?"

"Yes! Though, I mean, isn't that—"

"What about Federalized universal catastrophic health insurance that could backstop private plans and stabilize the market by capping the loss that an insurance company could take on an individual patient at something like a few million dollars a year?" the crow mused, kicking his head back and choking down the last few lumps of fish.

"I guess . . . So we're talking about health care policy?"

"I mean, you have to talk health care if you want to make American workers competitive globally. You have to start somewhere, right?" He unfolded a piece of shiny foil paper with some more notes on it. "Oh yeah, maybe we could bail out local journalism, too. Implement a tax like the U.K. does with television licenses that fund the BBC. Money would go into an account controlled by the individual that could be spent on subscriptions to newspapers and so on, online or print or maybe even TV stations. Of course then we'd have to think about campaign finance regulation. It's so perverse, the cost of advertising on TV is the biggest expense for most campaigns, which is why fund-raising is so—"

"Yeah, okay, just hold that thought. This is kind of big-picture stuff, I want to write it down in a different notebook."

"I don't have much time. I come to you from beyond the—"

"You are being really loud."

"Yes."

"Come to my room."

"Okay."

"First I have to hit the head, do you mind?"

"No."

I flipped each bottle up for the last drops of vino as I shimmied out of the booth. The train lurched side to side as I made my way to the can. The crow hopped along table to table leaving a mess of feathers and shattered saltshakers in front of my oblivious fellow passengers. In the bathroom, I splashed water on my face. He waited for me outside, preening and muttering, then perched on my shoulder as I ambled clumsily through two coach cars to the sliding door in the sleeper that opened to my sea green bunkbed and rusty sink. (My thanks to the porter for a timely turndown!)

The crow got comfortable in the bottom bunk. The lights out the window whizzed by. He continued to lecture me about professional sports, CBD oil, understanding the conflicts in Syria and Sudan as climate wars, the pros and cons of the latest generation of VR headsets, and the impossibility of retaining a modern level of technical sophistication in the event of a true civilization-ending cataclysm because all the easily obtained fossil fuels have already been exhausted during the current age. I was starting to dose off.

"Is there anything to be hopeful about?" I asked from the top bunk.

"Well," the crow said, "fewer people are living in extreme poverty than at any time in human history, armed conflict is at an historical low all over the world, population growth is close to a sustainable equilibrium, and with any luck some combination of environmental regulation, green energy, nuclear power, biointensive farming, and maybe even a quantum leap in carbon capture technology could save us from the worst effects of climate change. Then, with things stabilized, a generation born after the dawn of the digital age might get bored with ubiquitous consumer connectivity the same way the novelty of automobiles and then television wore off for each previous generation's grandchildren. Then they might rediscover community and empathy as essential components of a human life and have a chance to revitalize civilization at the individual, communal, and eventually global level so that your species can pursue some greater purpose that you and I can't even imagine."

"Do you think that will happen?"

"Could be."

"Well, that makes me feel better," I said.

"Good."

Then the great crow flapped up to rest his weight on my berth. He trained all seven of his eyes on mine, unhinged his beak with a loud crack, and gave me the worst blow job of my life.

Acknowledgments

Unlike our president, who takes all the credit for himself, I would like to acknowledge the extraordinary work and support of others who buttressed the making of *American Tantrum*.

This book wouldn't exist without the tireless efforts and extreme patience of our writing assistant Becca Scheuer. Becca's incredible note-taking, humor, and skill allowed us to envision the book early on.

My editor at William Morrow/HarperCollins, the extremely intelligent and patient Peter Hubbard (you'll notice a theme of patience, mostly because I'm bad with deadlines!). Peter gave me the room to create exactly the book I wanted to write, and his wisdom was vital. I want to thank the rest of the Morrow team: Liate Stehlik, Lynn Grady, publicist Sharyn Rosenblum, Nick Amphlett, Mumtaz Mustafa (who designed the book's fabulous cover), and all the behind-the-scenes folks who managed the production of the book, including Nyamekye Waliyaya, Andrea Molitor, and Bill Ruoto, my interior designer.

I want to thank the Casey family for producing Neil Casey so that we could become close friends at UCB, then roommates and comedy partners, and ultimately write this very book over dozens of cups of coffee in various hotel suites around Los Angeles.

I want to thank my beautiful, talented mother, Marlena; my stepfather, Stephen; and my father, Larry, who have always supported me and believed in me and all have incredible senses of humor and taste.

My wife, Flossie, who is a far more talented writer than I will ever be. I love her with all my heart.

Thank you to Sabiha and Geoffrey Arend for letting be a part of their family.

Thank you to my assistant and sister in law, or assistant in law, Emily Arend, who is also damned funny and has to deal with my inability to focus on a daily basis.

Everyone who worked on, or around, *The President Show*. We all know what we made and that it will stand the test of time.

A big thank-you to my team at 3Arts: Richard Abate, who is cooler than I can ever try to be, and my extremely talented and kind manager, Olivia Gerke, who has suffered through years of trying to decipher my confusing emails or weathering my insecurities as an actor and creator.

And to all my various pets from throughout my life, Birdy, Tootie, Mr. Chips, and Lulu.

About the Authors

ANTHONY ATAMANUIK can be seen as the host/"President Trump" on Comedy Central's *The President Show*. Anthony has been performing at the Upright Citizens Brigade Theatre in New York for seventeen years. He recurred on *30 Rock* as "Anthony" and recently appeared on *Difficult People* (Hulu), *Broad City* (Comedy Central), and *Tracey Breaks the News* (BBC One). Additionally, he wrote for the series *Time Traveling Bong* on Comedy Central. Selected as one of *Variety*'s 2016 Comics to Watch, he has received critical acclaim and acquired a fervent new fan base with his pitch-perfect Donald Trump impression, which has also been featured heavily on *The Howard Stern Show*. Anthony can be seen in the upcoming final season of *Unbreakable Kimmy Schmidt*. He is a WGA Award nominee for his work on season 1 of *The President Show*.

NEIL CASEY is an actor, writer, and proud member of the Writers Guild of America and the Screen Actors Guild. He has written for *Saturday Night Live, Inside Amy Schumer, Kroll Show, Mystery Science Theater 3000*, and *The President Show*, and appeared in *Ghostbusters, A Futile and Stupid Gesture, Silicon Valley, Curb Your Enthusiasm*, and *The President Show*.